Evidence-Based Instruction in Reading

A Professional Development Guide to Response to Intervention

Robin Wisniewski

Baldwin-Wallace College

Nancy D. Padak

Kent State University

Timothy V. Rasinski

Kent State University

Boston   Columbus   Indianapolis   New York   San Francisco   Upper Saddle River
Amsterdam   Cape Town   Dubai   London   Madrid   Milan   Munich   Paris   Montreal   Toronto
Delhi   Mexico City   São Paulo   Sydney   Hong Kong   Seoul   Singapore   Taipei   Tokyo

Vice President, Editor-in-Chief: Aurora Martínez Ramos
Editorial Assistant: Meagan French
Marketing Manager: Amanda Stedke
Marketing Manager: Danae April
Photo Research: Annie Pickert
Managing Editor: Central Publishing
Operations Specialist: Laura Messerly
Art Director: Jayne Conte
Cover Designer: Karen Salzbach
Cover Image: Getty Images
Project Managment: Saraswathi Muralidhar
Composition: PreMediaGlobal
Printer/Binder: Courier/Stoughton
Cover Printer: Courier/Stoughton
Text Font: 11/13 Giovanni Book

Wisniewski, Robin.
   Evidence-based instruction in reading : a professional development guide to response to intervention / Robin Wisniewski, Nancy D. Padak, Timothy V. Rasinski.
      p. cm.
   Includes bibliographical references.
   ISBN-13: 978-0-13-702255-7
   ISBN-10: 0-13-702255-7
   1. Reading (Elementary)—United States.   2. Response to intervention (Learning disabled children)
I. Padak, Nancy.   II. Rasinski, Timothy V.   III. Title.
   LB1573.W5746 2011
   372.41'6—dc22

                                                                    2010040758

10 9 8 7 6 5 4 3 2 1

www.pearsonhighered.com

ISBN-10: 0-13-702255-7
ISBN-13: 978-0-13-702255-7

Among us, we have been teachers and teacher educators for nearly 100 years! During this time, we have developed deep and abiding respect for teachers and trust in their ability to offer their students the very best possible instruction. Yet we also agree with librarian John Cotton Dana (1856–1929), who said, "Who dares to teach must never cease to learn."

Our careers have been marked by continual learning. We dedicate this book to all who have taught us and all whom we have taught— all who have dared to teach.

RW
NP
TR

About the Authors

Robin Wisniewski is an assistant professor of education at Baldwin-Wallace College, where she is Director of the Leadership in Higher Education graduate program. As a licensed psychologist and nationally certified school psychologist, her major interests, specialties, and teaching areas are the psychology of learning and leadership. She frequently works with teachers and school leaders and has taught and led over 200 courses, workshops, and presentations in various areas such as standardized and authentic assessment, program evaluation and research, diversity and cultural responsiveness, psychology and counseling, K–12 and college literacy, educational leadership, and curriculum development.

A graduate of Kent State University, Robin earned bachelor's degrees in business and psychology, an MEd and EdS in school psychology, a PhD in curriculum and instruction, and an Equivalency Doctorate in school psychology.

Nancy D. Padak is a distinguished professor in the Department of Teaching, Leadership and Curriculum Studies at Kent State University. She also directs the Reading and Writing Center at Kent State and teaches undergraduate and graduate courses in the area of literacy education. Prior to her arrival at Kent State in 1985, she was a classroom teacher and district administrator (language arts, reading, Title I) for the Elgin (Illinois) Schools.

Nancy has authored and edited books and monographs, has contributed book chapters, and has written more than 100 articles on topics related to literacy development. She is a frequent presenter at professional meetings and an active consultant for school districts within Ohio and in other parts of the Midwest. Nancy has also served in a variety of leadership roles in professional organizations, including the presidency of the College Reading Association, and as coeditor of *The Reading Teacher*, the *Journal of Literacy Research*, and the *Ohio Journal of English Language Arts*.

Timothy V. Rasinski is a professor of literacy education at Kent State University. He has written over 200 articles and has authored, coauthored, or edited over 50 books or curriculum programs on reading education. His scholarly interests include reading fluency and word study, reading in the elementary and middle grades, and readers who struggle. His research on reading has been cited by the National Reading Panel and has been published in journals such as *Reading Research Quarterly*, *The Reading Teacher*, *Reading Psychology*, and the *Journal of Educational Research*. Tim is currently writing the fluency chapter for Volume IV of the *Handbook of Reading Research*.

Recently, Tim served a three-year term on the Board of Directors of the International Reading Association, and from 1992 to 1999, he was coeditor of *The Reading Teacher*, the world's most widely read journal of literacy education. He has also served as coeditor of the *Journal of Literacy Research*. He is past president of the College Reading Association and has won the A. B. Herr and Laureate Awards from the College Reading Association for his scholarly contributions to literacy education.

Prior to coming to Kent State, Tim taught literacy education at the University of Georgia. He taught for several years as an elementary and middle school classroom and Title I teacher in Nebraska.

Contents

Series Introduction

Evidence-Based Instruction in Reading: A Professional Development Guide

Better than a thousand days of diligent study is one day spent with a great teacher.

JAPANESE PROVERB

*L*earning to read is perhaps a young child's greatest school accomplishment. Of course, reading is the foundation for success in all other school subjects. Reading is critical to a person's own intellectual development, later economic success, and the pleasure that is to be found in life.

Similarly, teaching a child to read is one of the greatest accomplishments a teacher can ever hope for. And yet reading and teaching reading are incredibly complex activities. The reading process involves elements of a person's psychological, physical, linguistic, cognitive, emotional, and social world. Teaching reading, of course, involves all these and more. Teachers must orchestrate the individuality of each child they encounter; the physical layout of the classroom and attendant materials; their own colleagues, parents, and school administration; the school's specified curriculum; and their own style of teaching! The popular cliché that "teaching reading is not rocket science" perhaps underestimates the enormity of the task of teaching children to read.

The complexity of teaching reading can be, quite simply, overwhelming. How does a teacher teach the various skills in reading to the point of mastery, while simultaneously attending to the school and state curricular guidelines, using an appropriate variety of materials, and meeting the individual needs of all children in the classroom?

X
....
SERIES
INTRODUCTION

*Evidence-Based
Instruction in
Reading*

We think that it was because of the enormous complexity of this task that many teachers resorted to prepackaged reading programs to provide the structure and sequence for a given grade level. Basal reading programs, for example, provide some assurance that at least some of the key skills and content for reading are covered within a given period of time.

The problem with prepackaged programs is that they are not sensitive to the culture of the classroom, school, and community; the individual children in the classroom; and the instructional style of the teacher. The one-size-fits-all approach adopted by such programs—with, of course, the best of intentions—resulted in programs that met the minimal needs of the students, that lacked the creative flair that only a teacher can give a program, and that absolved teachers of a good deal of the accountability for teaching their students. If children failed to learn to read, it was the fault of the program.

The fact of the matter is that many children failed to learn to read up to expectations using prepackaged programs. The results of periodic assessments of U.S. students' reading achievement, most notably the National Assessment of Educational Progress, have demonstrated little, if any, growth in student reading achievement over the past 30 years. This lack of growth in literacy achievement is at least partially responsible for equally dismal results in student growth in other subject areas that depend highly on a student's ability to read.

The National Reading Panel Report

Having noticed this disturbing trend, the National Reading Panel (NRP) was formed by the U.S. Congress in 1996 and given the mandate of reviewing the scientific research related to reading and determining those areas that science has shown have the greatest promise for improving reading achievement in the elementary grades. In 2000, the NRP came out with its findings. Essentially, the panel found that the existing scientific research points to five particular areas of reading that have the greatest promise for increasing reading achievement: phonemic awareness, phonics and word decoding, reading fluency, vocabulary, and reading comprehension. Additionally, the NRP indicated that investments in teachers, through professional development activities, hold promise for improving student reading achievement.

The findings of the NRP have been the source of considerable controversy, yet they have been used by the federal and state governments as well as by local school systems to define and mandate reading instruction. In particular, the federal Reading First program has mandated that any school receiving funds from Reading First must embed within its reading curriculum direct and systematic teaching of phonemic awareness, phonics, reading fluency, vocabulary, and comprehension. The intent of the mandate, of course, is to provide instruction that is based on the best evidence of a positive impact on students' reading achievement.

Although we may argue about certain aspects of the findings of the NRP—in particular, what it left out of its report on effective instructional principles—we find ourselves in solid agreement with the panel that the five elements that it identified are indeed critical to success in learning to read.

Phonemic awareness is crucial to early reading development. Students must develop an ability to think about the sounds of language and to manipulate those sounds in various ways—to blend sounds, to segment words into sounds, and so on. An inability to deal with language sounds in this way will set the stage for difficulty in phonics and word decoding. To sound out a word, which is essentially what phonics requires of students, readers must have adequate phonemic awareness. Yet some estimates indicate that as many as 20% of young children in the United States do not have sufficient phonemic awareness to profit fully from phonics instruction.

Phonics, or the ability to decode written words in text, is clearly essential for reading. Students who are unable to accurately decode at least 90% of the words they encounter while reading will have difficulty gaining appropriate meaning from what they read. We prefer to expand the notion of phonics to word decoding. Phonics, or using the sound–symbol relationship between letters and words, is, without doubt, an important way to decipher unknown words. However, there are other methods by which to decode written words. These include attending to the prefixes, suffixes, and base elements of longer words; examining words for rimes (word families) and other letter patterns; using meaningful context to determine unknown words; dividing longer words into smaller parts through syllabication; and making words part of one's sight vocabulary, those words that are recognized instantly and by sight. Good readers are able to employ all of these strategies and more. Appropriately, instruction needs to be aimed at helping students develop proficiency in learning to decode words using multiple strategies.

Reading fluency refers to the ability to read words quickly, as well as accurately, and with appropriate phrasing and expression. Fluent readers are able to decode words so effortlessly that they can

xii

SERIES
INTRODUCTION

*Evidence-Based
Instruction in
Reading*

direct their cognitive resources away from the low-level decoding task and toward the more important meaning-making or comprehension part of reading. For a long time, fluency was a relatively neglected area of the reading curriculum. In recent years, however, educators have come to realize that, although fluency deals with the ability to efficiently and effortlessly decode words, it is critical to good reading comprehension and needs to be part of any effective reading curriculum.

Word and concept meaning is the realm of *vocabulary*. Not only must readers be able to decode or sound out words, but also they must know what these words mean. Instruction aimed at expanding students' repertoire of word meanings and deepening their understanding of already known words is essential to reading success. Thus, vocabulary instruction is an integral part of an effective instructional program in reading.

Accurate and fluent decoding of words, coupled with knowledge of word meanings, may seem to ensure *comprehension*. However, there is more to it than that. Good readers also actively engage in constructing meaning, beyond individual words, from what they read. That is, they engage in meaning-constructing strategies while they read. These include ensuring that readers employ their background knowledge for the topics they encounter in reading. It also means that they ask questions, make predictions, and create mental images while they read. Additionally, readers monitor their reading comprehension and know when to stop and check things out when things begin to go awry—that is, when readers become aware that they are not making adequate sense out of what they are reading. These are just some of the comprehension strategies and processes good readers use while they read to ensure that they understand written texts. These same strategies must be introduced and taught to students in an effective reading instruction program.

Phonemic awareness, phonics/decoding, reading fluency, vocabulary, and comprehension are the five essential elements of effective reading programs identified by the NRP. We strongly agree with the findings of the panel—these elements must be taught to students in their reading program.

Rather than getting into in-depth detail on research and theory related to these topics, our intent in this series is to provide you with a collection of simple, practical, and relatively easy-to-implement instructional strategies, proven through research and actual practice, for teaching each of the five essential components. We think you will find the books in this series readable and practical. Our hope is that you will use these books as a set of handbooks for developing more effective and engaging reading instruction for all your students.

xiii
....
SERIES
INTRODUCTION
*Evidence-Based
Instruction in
Reading*

Professional Development in Literacy

Effective literacy instruction requires teachers to be knowledgeable, informed professionals capable of assessing student needs and responding to those needs with an assortment of instructional strategies. Whether you are new to the field or a classroom veteran, ongoing professional development is imperative. Professional development influences instructional practices that, in turn, affect student achievement (Wenglinsky, 2000). Effective professional development is not simply an isolated program or activity; rather, it is an ongoing, consistent learning effort where links between theoretical knowledge and the application of that knowledge to daily classroom practices are forged in consistent and meaningful ways (Renyi, 1998).

Researchers have noted several characteristics of effective professional development: It must be grounded in research-based practices; it must be collaborative, allowing teachers ample opportunities to share knowledge, as well as teaching and learning challenges, among colleagues; and it must actively engage teachers in assessing, observing, and responding to the learning and development of their students (Darling-Hammond & McLaughlin, 1995). This professional development series, *Evidence-Based Instruction in Reading: A Professional Development Guide*, is intended to provide a road map for systematic, participatory professional development initiatives.

Using the Books

Each of the first five books in the *Evidence-Based Instruction in Reading* series addresses one major component of literacy instruction identified by the National Reading Panel and widely accepted in the field as necessary for effective literacy programs: phonemic awareness, phonics, fluency, vocabulary, and comprehension. These five components are not, by any means, the only components needed for effective literacy instruction. Access to appropriate reading materials, productive home–school connections, and a desire to

xiv
....
SERIES
INTRODUCTION

*Evidence-Based
Instruction in
Reading*

learn to read and write are also critical pieces of the literacy puzzle, as are plans for working with students who struggle in reading. It is our hope, however, that by focusing in depth on each of the five major literacy components, we can provide educators and professional development facilitators with concrete guidelines and suggestions for enhancing literacy instruction. Our hope is that teachers who read, reflect, and act on the information in these books will be more able to provide effective instruction in each of the five essential areas of reading.

Each book is intended to be used by professional development facilitators, be they administrators, literacy coaches, reading specialists, and/or classroom teachers, and by program participants as they engage in professional development initiatives or in-service programs within schools or school districts. The use of the series can be adapted to meet the specific needs and goals of a group of educators. For example, a school may choose to hold a series of professional development sessions on each of the five major components of literacy instruction; it may choose to focus in depth on one or two components that are most relevant to its literacy program; or it may choose to focus on specific aspects, such as assessment or instructional strategies, of one or more of the five areas.

The books may also be useful in professional book club settings. An icon, included at spots for book club discussion, mark times when you might wish to share decisions about your own classroom to get colleagues' feedback. You might also want to discuss issues or solve problems with colleagues. Appendix A lists several other possible book club activities. These are listed by chapter and offer opportunities to delve into issues mentioned in the chapters in greater depth. It is important that, in collaboration with teachers, professional development needs be carefully addressed so that the appropriate content can be selected to meet those needs.

Overview of Book Content

To begin each book in the series, Chapter 1 presents a literature review that defines the literacy component to be addressed in that book, explains why this component is important in the context of a complete and balanced literacy program, and synthesizes key research findings that underlie the recommendations for evidence-based instructional practices that follow in subsequent chapters. The conclusion of Chapter 1 invites professional development program participants to analyze, clarify, extend, and discuss the material presented in this chapter.

Chapter 2 begins by presenting broad themes for effective assessment such as focusing on critical information, looking for patterns of behavior, recognizing developmental progressions, deciding how much assessment information is needed, using instructional situations for assessment purposes, using assessment information to guide instruction, and sharing assessment information with children and families. At the end of Chapter 2, professional development participants are asked to evaluate their current assessment practices, draw conclusions about needed change, and develop plans for change. The conclusion of the chapter provides vignettes and questions designed to generate collaborative discussion about and concrete ways to enhance connections between assessment and classroom instruction.

Chapter 3 outlines general principles for instruction. Participants are asked to evaluate their own instructional practices and to plan for refinement of those practices based on their students' needs. Each suggested instructional strategy in this chapter is based on the research presented in Chapter 1 and includes the purpose, necessary materials, and procedures for implementation. Ideas for engaging professional development participants in extended discussions related to phonemic awareness, phonics, fluency, vocabulary, or comprehension are offered at the end of Chapter 3.

Chapter 4 invites participants to think beyond classroom-based strategies by examining activities that can be recommended to families to support children's development of phonemic awareness, phonics, fluency, vocabulary, and comprehension at home. The final chapter provides a variety of print and Web-based resources to support instruction in phonemic awareness, phonics, fluency, vocabulary, or comprehension.

Together, the information and activities included in these books, whether used as is or selectively, will foster careful consideration of research-based practice. Professional development participants will learn about the research that supports their current practices and will be guided to identify areas for improvement in their classroom programs.

The need for new programs and methods for teaching reading is questionable. What is without question is the need for great teachers of reading—teachers who are effective, inspiring, and knowledgeable of children and reading. This series of books is our attempt to guide teachers to a deeper understanding of their craft and art—to help already good teachers become the great teachers that we need.

Introduction

Response to Intervention

*T*hink back to a time in your schooling when you had a learning difficulty. What was that like for you? Who helped you overcome the learning difficulty? Teachers? Family members? Friends? How did these people help you? Typically, it's difficult for us to relate our own learning challenges to those of our students who struggle with reading. Indeed, most of us are good readers.

Yet students with learning difficulties have been a focus of teaching for many years—specifically, since the Education of All Handicapped Children Act (EHA, 1975) called for special instruction for those with reading skills significantly below those of their peers. However, the responsibility for this instruction rested on teachers of special education rather than teachers in the general classroom. The 1990 reauthorization of the EHA as the Individuals with Disabilities Education Act (IDEA) focused on inclusion of special education students in the general classroom, therefore increasing the joint responsibilities of general education and special education teachers. Both sets of teachers, however, have seen a substantial overlap in reading needs between students who struggle with reading and those who are diagnosed with learning disabilities (Reid & Lienemann, 2006; Snow, Griffin, & Burns, 2005; Stanovich & Siegal, 1994).

The number of students diagnosed with learning disabilities has risen threefold since 1975, and students with learning disabilities now constitute at least half of all children in special education (U.S. Department of Education, 2005). Researchers have noted that the rise in diagnoses may reflect an over-identification of learning disabilities and could be averted with targeted classroom instruction for students with special needs in reading. In fact, targeted instruction is the focus of the most recent reauthorization of IDEA in 2004.

This instruction—where students with special needs in your classroom receive more attention and monitoring in five aspects of reading instruction (National Reading Panel, 2000): phonemic awareness, phonics/decoding, fluency, vocabulary, and comprehension—is the cornerstone of this book. Students who do not respond to the interventions may have learning disabilities in reading.

Before you begin this professional development program, we invite you to consider and discuss with colleagues the following items, which might help you to frame your interpretation and application of the material in this book. Take some time now to write notes about these aspects of your literacy instruction, particularly with regard to learners with special needs. Share your answers with colleagues.

- Describe the conditions under which you teach and your students learn.

  _____

  _____

  _____

- What do your students read?

  _____

  _____

  _____

- Describe the major goals of your reading program.

  _____

  _____

  _____

- What are the principles that ground or serve as a rationale for your program?

  _____

  _____

  _____

- Describe in your daily schedule where you focus on the five reading elements:
  - Phonemic awareness
  - Phonics
  - Fluency

- Vocabulary
- Comprehension

- How do you define or describe the students with special needs in your classroom? Students with disabilities who are included in your classroom? Struggling readers? Students who are at risk for reading difficulty?

  _____

  _____

  _____

- How do you provide instruction for students with special needs in reading?

  _____

  _____

  _____

- How do you involve parents in your literacy program?

  _____

  _____

  _____

- How do you currently assess student progress in reading?

  _____

  _____

  _____

- How do you currently assess the reading progress of students with special needs?

  _____

  _____

  _____

The chapters that follow provide an organizational framework for making instructional decisions for students who have special needs in reading. In particular, we focus on identifying effective elements of instruction and offering suggestions for instructional modifications in the general education classroom. Our focus is on elementary classrooms; as Brozo (2009–2010) notes, little research is currently available on the use of Response to Intervention (RTI) in upper grades. Thus, if you are a middle school or high school teacher, we invite you to consider how information in this book could be adapted for your classroom.

The issues we address provide research-based perspectives on questions general education teachers frequently ask us. We encourage those interested in a broader and deeper look at these issues, such as consideration of outside-the-general-education-classroom support, to consult some of the resources listed in Chapter 5 under "RTI and Students with Special Needs in Reading"—particularly Allington (2008); Lyons (2003); Rasinski, Padak, and Fawcett (2010); and Strickland, Ganske, and Monroe (2002).

Chapter 1 presents an overview of current research and professional literature. Research-based answers are provided for questions such as who learners with special needs are, why a focus on learners with special needs is important, and how instruction can be most effective. The end of the chapter invites you to analyze, clarify, extend, discuss, and apply information learned from this chapter.

Chapter 2 focuses on assessment and begins by describing broad truisms of assessment that can be applied to all aspects of literacy learning and that work particularly well for reading assessment for students with special needs. After working with these broad assessment ideas, you are asked to examine more closely your own current assessment practices in terms of both critical aspects of assessment of the reading elements and how you assess individual students with special needs. Several assessment ideas are described.

Chapter 3 focuses on research-based instructional practices. General principles for literacy instruction for learners with special needs are presented first. Then you are asked to complete a semantic feature analysis to evaluate your own instructional practices, considering both instructional practices that are effective and those that are in need of fine-tuning. The strategy suggestions that follow have been adapted for targeted instruction and are related to suggestions provided in the first five books of the series: phonemic awareness, phonics, fluency, vocabulary, and comprehension.

Chapter 4 moves beyond classroom-based strategies and considers recommendations for how to help parents with at-home activities in all of the elements of reading. Helping parents to understand special needs and special education is also addressed in this chapter. Some basic recommendations for English language learners are provided as well, although a separate book in this series (Wisniewski, Fawcett, Padak, & Rasinski, in press) offers a great deal more information about this important group of readers.

Chapter 5 provides instructional and professional resources for teaching students with special needs in reading. Several charts to help you use information from this book in your own classroom are also presented.

Throughout the book, you will find ample room to make notes about various aspects of planning and implementing effective instruction for students with special needs. We encourage you to use these spaces to record insights and ideas that are particularly pertinent to your own instruction. Doing so should provide you with the kind of concrete plan of action you'll need to offer students more consistent and effective opportunities to develop their reading.

Learners with Special Needs: What Does the Research Tell Us?

2
....
CHAPTER 1

*Learners with
Special Needs:
What Does the
Research Tell Us?*

*T*he first graders in Ms. Fernandez's classroom were practicing their reading comprehension with the book *A Charlie Brown Thanksgiving* (Schultz, 2002). After reading the book to the class, Ms. Fernandez asked different students about the characters, the setting, and the order in which events happened. Many students in the class could retell the story sequentially. However, Ms. Fernandez noticed one student, Lacey, who had difficulty with the retelling.

"The story is about Charlie Brown and Thanksgiving dinner," Lacey said.

"What happened first in the story?" Ms. Fernandez asked.

"They had dinner and his friends were coming over?" questioned Lacey, selecting two events that she had heard during the oral reading of the story.

Ms. Fernandez was familiar with Lacey's reading comprehension. In fact, she assessed Lacey's reading when the year started and found that Lacey could look at pictures, pick out some words, and tell the gist of a story. Lacey's reading skills were considered "emergent," whereas most of the students in her class were more advanced, in the category of "beginning" reading.

Ms. Fernandez's plan for the beginning readers in her class was to use evidence-based reading strategies in phonemic awareness, phonics, fluency, vocabulary, and comprehension (National Reading Panel, 2000). The instructional strategies she chose are from the first five books in the *Evidence-Based Instruction in Reading* series and included a three-day rime routine for phonemic awareness and phonics practice, word predictions, fluency development lessons, and story predictions.

However, Lacey, as well as a small percentage of other students in Ms. Fernandez's class, needs more scaffolding and support with some of these strategies in order to gain reading skills similar to those of her peers. Lacey, along with about 10 to 15% of the other students in Ms. Fernandez's class, has special needs.

Who Are Learners with Special Needs?

Think about when you have heard the term *special needs*. Most likely, special needs brings to mind *learning disability*, but other thoughts may come to mind as well, like students who struggle with reading. These students are probably the ones who learn letter–sound relationships more slowly than do their peers. Perhaps they read fewer words orally from common word lists than do their peers. Perhaps their *ability* to learn appears even with that of their peers, but they lag in gaining reading *skills* that meet age-level expectations.

All of the children described above have special needs in reading, but some are simply struggling readers and others have learning disabilities in reading. Both groups have similar reading needs, but they may also respond differently to classroom reading instruction or interventions. That is, they have different *responses to intervention.*

Response to Intervention, or RTI, is an approach to delivery of instruction, or *intervention* in the schools (National Association of State Directors of Education [NASDE], 2006). The interventions used in RTI have three levels of intensity for different students who have different challenges in learning to read. The first level or tier is for the majority (about 75–80%) of students in the classroom. These children receive and benefit from universal instruction. The second level or tier is for a smaller percentage (10–15%) of students in the classroom; these children receive more targeted instruction because the universal instruction provided in the first tier did not enable them to be successful. The third level or tier includes the smallest percentage (5–10%) of students, those who are not responding sufficiently to interventions in the second tier. (Throughout this book, we refer to these levels as Tier 1, Tier 2, and Tier 3.)

Think of Tier 2 interventions as instructional adaptations that a general education teacher can reasonably accomplish (Fuchs & Fuchs, 1998). Adaptations may include extra instructional materials such as concrete visual scaffolds, small-group instruction focused on areas of need, or adjustments in support provided for students. In Ms. Fernandez's class, Lacey would be considered to be in Tier 2, or to be one of 10–15% of students in her class who needs targeted instruction—and, according to RTI, if Lacey's reading progress does not improve as a result of this targeted instruction, she may be considered for Tier 3, or the most intensive interventions.

Who are students with special needs? They comprise those who have fewer reading skills than do their peers, gain new reading skills more slowly than do their peers, and/or have achievement scores in reading that are lower than their own ability suggests they should be (e.g., Vaughn & Fuchs, 2003). The goal of instruction is to gain reading skills, of course, but evidence-based instruction for students with special needs—that is, Tier 2 instruction—aims to narrow the reading gap between these students and their Tier 1 peers.

Why Is It Important to Focus on Learners with Special Needs?

Part of the answer to this question is evident in the definition just provided: It is important to focus on learners with special needs because they will likely respond to interventions, therefore gaining reading skills, raising their levels of achievement, and diminishing the extent to which they struggle with reading throughout the remainder of their school years. In fact, research that focuses on targeted interventions and progress monitoring of students with special needs in the regular classroom indicates better attendance, higher achievement scores, reduced difficulties in future grades, improved social skills, and fewer misdiagnoses of learning disabilities (Demeris, Childs, & Jordan, 2007; Rea, McLaughlin, & Walther-Thomas, 2002).

Unfortunately, studies have also found that without appropriate intervention and response in the regular classroom, a disproportionate number of students will be classified with learning disabilities. A 2005 report from the U.S. Department of Education shows that students with learning disabilities constitute 5.4% of the total school population and approximately half of the population of students with disabilities among school-aged students. These numbers have more than tripled since 1975, when the Education for All Handicapped Children Act (EHA), now the Individuals with Disabilities Education Act (IDEA), was enacted.

These increases in disability diagnoses have caused educators and others to place the process used to diagnose learning disabilities under a microscope. Historically, diagnosis of a learning disability is based on the "discrepancy formula"; thus, a child is considered likely to have a learning disability when his or her scores on individual achievement tests are significantly lower than his or her individual scores on ability, or IQ, tests. When this significant discrepancy exists between a child's reading achievement and ability scores and he or she is progressing more slowly in reading than are grade-level peers, a learning disability in reading is the diagnosis.

Notice that the diagnosis tells us only that the student's actual achievement scores are lower than the scores measuring his or her potential ability. It does not provide information about whether the student has a "true" disability or whether the student struggles with reading instruction that does not meet his or her needs. It does not tell us where to target our instruction and whether the targeted instruction could increase the student's reading achievement. Consider a student who did not have access to books before starting kindergarten.

Or another student whose parents speak a language other than English. Or yet another student who has not yet had sufficient time with evidence-based instruction in the regular classroom. These students will likely have low scores on reading achievement tests and may well struggle in the classroom. But their ability, or IQ, scores may be in the average range. Do they have a learning disability in reading because their reading achievement scores are significantly lower than their ability scores and they are not making progress in reading within their general education classrooms?

Not necessarily. Researchers assert that a diagnosis of learning disability is possible only for children who do not make progress after they receive appropriate, evidence-based instruction in their regular classrooms (e.g., see research reviews by Fuchs, 2003, and Gresham, 2002). And the federal government agrees. Instead of using discrepancy formulas as the only way to determine a disability, IDEA makes it possible to diagnose a learning disability in reading based on a child's response to classroom intervention, or RTI.

Why is it important to focus on learners with special needs? Research has shown that with the RTI model, struggling readers make progress in the general education classroom with Tier 2 interventions. Those who do not progress may or may not be considered as having learning disabilities unless more intensive Tier 3 interventions suggest internal, not instructional, reasons for their lack of progress. RTI, then, turns the focus of disability classification toward the classroom contexts, and therefore toward the responsibility of the regular classroom teacher to implement evidence-based reading instruction for all students, including those with special needs.

How Can I Help Learners with Special Needs Improve Their Reading?

The first steps in planning reading instruction for learners with special needs involve looking at your current emphasis in instruction on the elements of reading (phonemic awareness, phonics, fluency, vocabulary, and comprehension) and how you are currently meeting the needs of students with special needs in your classroom. These questions may help you assess your current practices:

- Is your instruction comprehensive? Does it cover all the essential elements of reading your students need?
- Is your instruction systematic?

6
....

CHAPTER 1

Learners with
Special Needs:
What Does the
Research Tell Us?

- How do you systematically teach the essential reading components?
- How do you differentiate your instruction to meet the particular needs of your students?
- What instructional routines enhance your instruction?
- How do you monitor the progress of your students who develop as readers at a slower rate than do other students in your classroom?
- How do you motivate your students?
- What peer reading work happens in your classroom?

Instruction for students with special needs depends on students' individual needs. In the next chapter, we describe several ways to assess students' needs in reading, and in each of the five previous books in the series, we go into individual assessment of phonemic awareness, phonics, fluency, vocabulary, and comprehension in more depth. Here we describe several methods for developing reading strengths among students with special needs.

Provide Comprehensive Instruction

We have learned that the best reading instruction involves several critical elements (phonemic awareness, phonics, fluency, vocabulary, and comprehension). Although your students may have specific needs in one or more of these areas, they also need instruction in all areas. Focusing on one area to the exclusion of others will likely cause reading problems in other areas. Effective instruction needs to include all elements of effective instruction, with particular emphasis on students' particular needs.

Provide Systematic Instruction

Students with special needs in reading deserve systematic instruction. Systematic instruction is a carefully thought out sequence of activities that will lead all students to a desired goal. No doubt you already think systematically while planning your reading lessons for each day. Adding targeted (or Tier 2) instruction to these plans is easy.

First, ensure that your regular lesson plans address both short-term instructional goals (What do you expect students to know or do at the end of the lesson?) and long-term instructional goals (How does this knowledge or behavior contribute to overall achievement in reading and the development of avid readers?). For example, when focusing on phonemic awareness, your short-term goal may be for students to add, delete, or change sounds in a given word to create new or rhyming words. Your long-term goal may be for students to develop phonemic awareness so that they can benefit from decoding instruction.

Second, analyze all students' skills related to the short-term goal. Pay particular attention to the skill levels of your students who are not quite getting it. For example, you could use a special phonemic awareness assessment such as the *Yopp–Singer Test of Phoneme Segmentation* (Yopp, 1995). Or you could observe how students respond to sound tasks (e.g., asking students to identify first sounds in selected words or an odd sound in a list of words).

Third, select strategies and materials to use with all students and with the students who are struggling. For example, for students who are not identifying letter–sound relationships, you could use animated videos to isolate sounds in familiar spoken words or invite children to work with partners or provide additional instruction or practice. In other words, adapt instruction to meet students' needs.

Finally, monitor the progress of the individual students for whom you adapted instruction. Find a way to gauge the impact of the adapted instruction. You might want to use a graph that represents the number of sounds the child is learning over a period of time, for example.

These steps are even more powerful when you teach students to be metacognitive. Metacognition is awareness of the learning goal, the strategies used, and the outcome of the strategies. Metacognitive awareness enables students to use new knowledge strategically, and thus to monitor their own learning (Montague, 2008; Mooney, Ryan, Uhing, Reid, & Epstein, 2005; Spencer & Logan, 2005). That is, they are more able to problem solve when approaching a difficult task.

You might want to experiment with student self-regulation by asking students what they will know by the end of a lesson. As you are providing instruction, you can ask students what the task is, what strategies they might use, and, after using the strategies, how well those strategies worked. At the end of the lesson, you can ask students what they learned and how this learning can help them in reading.

Encourage Social Interaction

Social interaction, another method associated with metacognition and self-regulation (Salonen, Vauras, & Efklides, 2005), should be an important component of your work with students with special

8
....

CHAPTER 1

*Learners with
Special Needs:
What Does the
Research Tell Us?*

needs. In fact, social interactions with others can create specific thinking structures (Palincsar, 1998). These structures are part of a child's learning, and the development occurs twice: "first, on a social level and later on the individual level; first between people (interpsychological) and then inside the child (intrapsychological)" (Vygotsky, 1978, p. 57).

In other words, children's thinking is first co-constructed between a child and another person, like a peer or an adult. Second, the thinking becomes internalized. For example, while working individually with a tutor, a child stumbles over the word *knowledge*. The tutor prompts the child to cover *ledge* in order to recognize *know*. Once the child recognizes *know*, then the tutor asks, "Where do you recall hearing the word *know*?" The child responds with a personal experience, the tutor says the word, and both say the word aloud together. Later, while reading aloud again, the child comes across the word *knowledge* and continues fluently through the sentence. In this example, the child internalized the vocabulary word *knowledge* after working with a prompt, question, and reinforcement from the tutor.

Prompts and questions are simple routines used when working one-on-one with a student to encourage student talk. Prompts may include the following:

- While I point to these pictures, tell me what words they represent.
- Tell me what words you know from this list and help me rewrite them on this sheet of paper.
- After I read this page, I will read part and then you will read part. Then we will read it together before you read it on your own.
- Tell me the beginning, middle, and end of this story, and I will write what you say in this graphic organizer.

These prompts work well for a variety of students, including those who do not seem open to talking and those who talk frequently but may be off task. This routine provides reinforcement for students as you listen and respond or add to what they say.

In addition to prompts, questions facilitate student talk. The types of questions, however, should be authentic and focus on higher-order thinking (Rasinski, Padak, & Fawcett, 2010). An authentic question is asked to truly know what another person is thinking. For example, when you ask, "Where do you recall hearing the word *know*?" like in the example above or "What does this story make you think of?" you want to know what is in the student's mind. These are also higher-order questions, as they ask the student to make connections or apply the story to some aspect of self, text, or world that is external to the story. Following are some examples of authentic, higher-order questions:

- What other words can you think of that begin with the *s* sound?
- Where do you recall using those words before?
- How do you think the daughter and mother in the story are alike? Different? Why?
- What do you think about the duck making her own home while the rest of the ducks flew south for the winter?

In addition to prompts and questions posed one-on-one with a child, there are useful strategies that structure student talk in groups. One such strategy is *think–pair–share*. The three steps in think–pair–share encourage students to think individually in order to activate background knowledge, promote student talk with a peer, and gather students' collective thoughts. Each step can be facilitated with a few moments of thinking and sharing before or during a reading activity.

Before you start the strategy, decide on its purpose within the lesson. Is the purpose to generate more vocabulary words? Or to make predictions about a story as a pre-reading comprehension activity? For example, if your purpose is to use prediction to improve comprehension, you might follow these steps:

1. Direct the students to think about the question "What is the book going to be about?" while looking at the book cover. Because step one is to "think" individually, you could help by telling them to take a few moments by themselves to write down words or draw a sketch about what they think might happen in the story.

2. Ask students to pair with peers next to them or partners that you have predetermined. Say, "Listen to your peer tell you about his or her prediction, and then share yours." To vary this step, you might ask students to compare their predictions: How are they similar? How are they different? You might also ask pairs to agree on a prediction that is unique or that has a particular personal or text connection.

3. Ask students to share their predictions with the group. Students could share their own or their peer's prediction, either by volunteering or by taking turns. You or a helper could record

10
....

CHAPTER 1

*Learners with
Special Needs:
What Does the
Research Tell Us?*

what students share so that all the students involved could see the individual predictions. You could also invite other members of the class to comment on the predictions, talk about why certain predictions do/don't make sense, and so forth.

In think–pair–share, peers encourage student talk. Several other methods for peer learning have shown promise for students with special needs, including such forms as classwide peer tutoring, reciprocal peer tutoring, group contingencies, and peer monitoring (Hoff & Robinson, 2002). These peer-mediated interventions, although specific in their implementation, have common threads: using peers as tutors, models, reinforcers, and managers of academic tasks. Once students have learned something, providing them with opportunities to share what they know with peers is a first step in creating peer tutoring structures. Peers can talk, learn to ask good questions, and encourage conversation, while also using scaffolds that are visual and concrete.

Use Concrete Visual Scaffolds

The National Reading Panel (2000) advocated for cognitive strategy instruction to help students be involved in their learning. Cognitive strategies that are visual improve the overall reading achievement of students with disabilities. Almost 40 years of research highlights such visual strategies as semantic organizers, framed outlines, and cognitive maps. Using these visual strategies improves the overall reading achievement of students with learning disabilities (Kim, Vaughn, Wanzek, & Wei, 2004). Sample graphic organizers are located in Chapter 3. In Chapter 5, we provide references to websites with a variety of visual strategies for you to use or adapt.

Visual strategies work best when students associate each strategy with the learning outcome. For example, if the learning outcome is to distinguish the beginning, middle, and ending sounds of words, pictures of common nouns can serve as a visual reference. Another example of a learning outcome is to list questions about essential elements from informational text (e.g., why, who, where, what, when, and how) and identify answers. The cognitive map could be a fishbone with six extensions, three on each side, that represent each essential question.

Even more powerful for contemporary children is the use of computer applications. For example, word processing programs contain word art and an array of fonts with which to create letters, words, their names, and even classmates' names. Internet sites such as http://www.readwritethink.org contain templates for trading cards and comic strips that are easy for children to use to create words or character perspectives from stories or nonfiction text.

Learners with special needs also benefit from visual strategies that are concrete. Concrete visual strategies are those that are multisensory—that is, they include more than one learning pathway to the brain (e.g., visual and tactile) (International Dyslexia Association, 2008). An example would be showing letter–sound relationships using playdough, sand, or shaving cream. Like all strategies, concrete visual strategies work best when students associate each strategy with the learning outcome. For identifying letter–sound relationships using action phonics (Cunningham, 1987), for example, students simulate *driving* in response to the blend *dr* or *twisting* in response the blend *tw*. Concrete objects that students can touch, such as magnetic letters, chips used for counting sounds in words, or word cards used for a word wall, are especially helpful.

Follow the Five Principles of RTI

All these ideas will be most effective when you bundle them into an RTI framework. Recall that RTI is an approach to delivery of instruction with three levels, or tiers, of intensity: least intense for most students, more intense for fewer students, and most intense for the fewest students. Tier 2, for about 10–15% of students, is the level where you can meet students' special needs in the general classroom.

When considering Tier 2 interventions, follow the five principles of RTI (Fuchs & Fuchs, 2005; NASDE, 2006). The first principle is to *be proactive and preventative*. Like analyzing student skills in systematic instruction, being proactive is noticing which students will need assistance and what their specific reading needs are. This will allow you to be preventative, since you will avoid unnecessary special education referrals by implementing and monitoring targeted classroom interventions for children who need them. Do your very best to ensure that instruction meets students' needs so that students have no opportunity to fail.

The second principle is to *ensure an instructional match among student skills, the curriculum, and instruction*. Focus your instructional attention on important aspects of reading growth. Look for areas where lack of understanding is hampering students' achievement in reading and is therefore making it difficult or impossible for students to achieve the broad curriculum goals that frame instruction.

12
....

CHAPTER 1

*Learners with
Special Needs:
What Does the
Research Tell Us?*

The third principle is to *use a problem-solving approach*. Problem solving uses data to make decisions on instruction. For example, if a student practices repeated readings and word recognition automaticity (as measured by words read per minute) is not increasing over a period of time, then another fluency strategy such as assisted reading (reading while listening to a fluent reading of the same text—e.g., using audio-recorded readings) may work instead.

The fourth principle is to *use effective practices*. Effective practices are evidence-based—that is, based on research that is presented in this book.

The fifth and last principle is to *incorporate a systems-level approach*. A systems-level approach is schoolwide. When a school adopts RTI as the approach to intervention, then monitoring a child's response to interventions becomes daily practice. With the daily practice also comes a common language of schoolwide reading improvement.

Professional Development Suggestions

ACED: Analysis, Clarification, Extension, Discussion

I. REFLECTION (10–15 minutes)

ANALYSIS

- What, for you, were the most interesting and/or important ideas in this introduction regarding students with special needs?

  _____

  _____

  _____

  _____

- What information was new to you?

  _____

  _____

  _____

  _____

CLARIFICATION

- Did anything surprise you? Confuse you?

  _____

  _____

  _____

  _____

EXTENSION

- What questions do you have?

  _____

  _____

  _____

  _____

14
....

CHAPTER 1

*Learners with
Special Needs:
What Does the
research Tell Us?*

II. DISCUSSION (20 minutes)

- Form groups of 4–6 members.
- Appoint a *facilitator (timer)* and *recorder.*
- Share responses. Make sure that each person has shared his or her responses to each category (Analysis/Clarification/Extension).
- Help each other with any areas of confusion.
- Answer and/or discuss questions raised by group members.
- On chart paper, the recorder should summarize the main discussion points and identify issues or questions the group would like to raise for general discussion.

III. APPLICATION (10 minutes)

- Based on your reflection and discussion, how might you apply what you have learned from the introduction regarding students with special needs?

_____

_____

_____

_____

This chapter describes several methods for developing reading strengths among students with special needs. One in particular is *encourage social interaction*. Teacher prompts, questions, and structures for peer interaction are ways to encourage student talk.

With your colleagues, make recommendations for improving student talk in your current instructional routines. First, think of prompts that you use in your classroom. Second, think of questions that you use. Third, think of instructional routines that incorporate student talk. With each of these, make recommendations to add to or enhance these prompts, questions, and structures.

Way to promote student talk	Examples of current prompts, questions, and structures	Recommendations for adding or enhancing prompts, questions, and structures
Prompts		
Questions		
Structures		

Follow the Five Principles of RTI

This chapter introduces RTI as an approach to the delivery of instruction that can be used as a framework for teaching reading to students with special needs. Recall the five principles of RTI. Work with colleagues to discover how you are currently involved with the five principles in your instruction. Then make recommendations that will enhance your use of each of the five principles. After working through this book with colleagues, you could also return to this chart and make adjustments to each column.

Five principles of RTI	How do we currently follow the principle?	How can we enhance following the principle?
Be proactive and preventative		
Ensure an instructional match among student skills, the curriculum, and instruction		
Use a problem-solving approach		
Use effective practices		
Incorporate a systems-level approach		

CHAPTER 2

Assessing Learners with Special Needs

17

*M*ost of this chapter is devoted to informal teacher assessments because we believe that you, as someone who is with your students day in and day out, are in the best position to determine how they are achieving in reading. However, because of the prevalence of standardized tests in today's schools, we would be remiss if we did not address that issue.

In the past decade, politicians and the general public have increasingly demanded "proof" that students are learning and that the quality of their education is high. In response, we have given students more and more tests, many required and some associated with "high-stakes" decisions such as student promotion or graduation, teacher merit pay, and school sanctions.

If your school, district, and/or state requires administration of certain tests related to reading, you may find these test results helpful in assessing your students as readers. Before using these results to make instructional decisions though, we advise you to consider what these tests really assess and what useful information they can provide. Is oral reading, as measured by the number of words a student reads correctly in a short period of time, enough to draw conclusions about the student as a reader (or does this result refer to one small aspect of the student's reading ability)? Suppose a student earned a stanine score of 2 or a percentile rank of 35 on a standardized reading test. What should you do to promote this student's reading achievement? We ask these questions because we believe that standardized test results aren't terribly useful for making instructional decisions, which is the core of developing effective support for struggling readers. So we urge you to temper your use of these test results with professional caution.

Big Ideas

In each of the books in the *Evidence-Based Instruction in Reading* series, we have identified several "big ideas" to guide your thinking about assessment. These big ideas apply to assessing all aspects of literacy learning (indeed, all aspects of learning), but the comments and examples below frame them in the context of assessing the progress of students with special needs. In particular, assessment should enable you to determine how these students are responding to the interventions that you choose for targeted instruction in phonemic awareness, phonics, fluency, vocabulary, and comprehension.

Focus on Critical Information

Aim for a direct connection between the assessment tools/strategies you use and what you need to know. You can decide about the critical information you need to know by considering the broad definitions of phonemic awareness, phonics, fluency, vocabulary, and comprehension presented in Chapter 3 in light of your own students. For example, if what you need to know is the child's progress in decoding words based on your phonics intervention, then you may choose a word recognition assessment tool. This tool could be a list of words common for that particular grade level (e.g., the Fry Instant Word List) or a list of first and last names in your classroom (i.e., the *Names Test*, found in this chapter).

It may also help to think about a student whom you find to be particularly good at the reading element you are targeting. Try making a list of his or her observable indicators. For the word recognition example, this list might include the following: What words did this student struggle with? What are "fix-up" strategies that he or she used with an unknown word? Having thought about the abstract definition of the particular element and your own students with special needs, then you can decide on critical information. McTighe and Wiggins (2004) suggest that this process works best when it begins at the end: (a) If the desired result is for learners to . . . , (b) then assessment should provide you with evidence of . . . , (c) so assessment tasks need to include something like. . . .

Look for Patterns of Behavior

Tierney (1998) notes that assessment "should be viewed as ongoing and suggestive, rather than fixed or definitive" (p. 385). No one instance can possibly tell you what you need to know about whether a child with special needs is responding to the intervention. Situations make a difference, as do practice, difficulty level of the material, and a host of other factors. So your goal should be to determine children's progress with reading by finding patterns of reading behavior. To do this, you need a plan.

Recall that interventions in Response to Intervention (RTI) have three levels of intensity for different percentages of children. In order to find out the different percentages in your classroom, get baseline information about all the children at the beginning of the year. Decide who are in the majority (about 75–80%) of students that will receive and benefit from Tier 1 or universal instruction. Then identify the children (about 10–15%) that are below this class baseline; these students may need Tier 2 interventions, which offer more targeted instruction, because the universal instruction provided in Tier 1 may not enable them to be successful. As the school year continues, your students in Tier 1 may need more targeted help, while your students in Tier 2 may be responding well to interventions and need less targeted help. Therefore, we suggest repeating this assessment process every few months.

As you develop your assessment plan and analyze students' reading abilities, you may find that some students are solidly in Tier 1 or Tier 2. That is, they may be progressing well across the board or appear to need assistance in all aspects of reading. Other students, however, may present more uneven profiles, such as decoding strengths coupled with comprehension weaknesses or fluency difficulties. Thus, as you use assessment results to plan instruction, you will probably need to differentiate instruction in particular aspects of reading for some individuals.

You need to develop some method of monitoring students' progress in reading throughout the school year. For example, you may choose to assess students quarterly. In addition to recording results for individual students in their portfolios, a class chart can be useful for summarizing these results so that you can use them to adjust instruction.

Recognize Children's Developmental Progressions (Can't, Can Sometimes, Can Always) and Cultural or Linguistic Differences

Tierney (1998) advises that "assessment should be more developmental and sustained than piecemeal and shortsighted" (p. 384). "I envision . . . assessments that build upon, recognize, and value rather than displace what students have experienced in their worlds" (p. 381). Your plans should be sensitive to both of these issues. With regard to the former issue, for example, children develop a general notion of reading before they are able to talk about its component parts, like decoding words and comprehending what they are reading. Likewise, they may be able to recognize aspects of the reading elements before they can produce them. For example, a child comprehends before reading independently and may develop a general notion of fluency before he or she is able to talk about its component parts (e.g., phrasing, prosody). With regard to the latter issue, cultural differences may influence some aspects of performance (e.g., eye contact), so it will be important to know about the nonverbals your students have learned at home and in their communities.

Be Parsimonious When Gathering Assessment Information

The question: How much assessment information do you need? The answer: You need only enough to help you make good instructional decisions. One way to conceptualize this quantity-of-information question is to recall the idea of RTI: three levels of intensity of instructional delivery for different percentages of children. Then, for assessment, think in terms of three related layers of assessment information, as shown in Figure 2.1.

Like Tier 1 instruction in RTI, the lowest level of Figure 2.1 relates to the majority of the students. Actually, it refers to assessment plans for *all* of the students, not just the majority. Begin with a broad plan to assess all students' reading at the beginning of the year and then perhaps quarterly. After each assessment cycle concludes, think about results: What (or whom) do you still have questions about? This is the point to move to the middle layer of the triangle, which is analogous to Tier 2 of RTI. Here you will do more targeted (and time-consuming) reading assessments. You might work individually with a student, perhaps doing

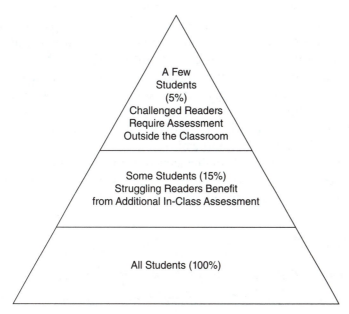

Figure 2.1   A Model for Classroom Assessment

Source: Rasinski, et al., *Teaching Children Who Find Reading Difficult,* Figure 2.4 "A Model for Classroom Assessment," p. 31, © 2008. Reproduced by permission of Pearson Education, Inc.

more of what you've already done or using a "deeper" assessment. Since these are the students who may need Tier 2 interventions, the purpose of the assessment is to guide instructional decision making.

For example, you might assess a student's fluency with easier material or in assisted situations (where you model fluent reading of the text and read it chorally with the student before asking him or her to read it alone). Or you might assess a student's comprehension with an oral retelling or a different text. If you still have questions, don't hesitate to ask for outside help. A student or two in the class may benefit from a diagnosis by a reading specialist or other highly specialized professional. Don't delay, and don't hesitate. Every lost day represents lost opportunities for that student's learning. Above all, keep assessments at these different layers related to one another and focused on the same key reading issues.

Use Instructional Situations for Assessment Purposes

Tierney (1998) notes that ideally "[a]ssessments should emerge from the classroom rather than be imposed upon it" (p. 375). We can think of two good reasons for this stance, one conceptual and the other practical. From a conceptual perspective, you want to know how students behave in typical instructional situations. After all, a major purpose of assessment is to provide instructional guidance. And practically, gathering assessment information from instruction saves time for your teaching and students' learning. Students don't learn much of value during testing sessions. To evaluate your reading instruction for possible assessment situations, you might begin by listing the instructional opportunities your students have to read. Then develop a plan to capture observations about their word recognition, fluency, and comprehension during instruction. Above all, take West's (1998) advice to heart: "I want instruction and evaluation to be in meaningful authentic contexts" (p. 550).

Include Plans for (a) Using Assessment Information to Guide Instruction and (b) Sharing Assessment Information With Students and Their Parents

The last step of your assessment planning might be to double-check ideas against their primary purposes: to help you teach more effectively and to communicate your insights with students and their parents. With regard to the former, it may be particularly important to think about how you can adjust instruction for Tier 2 students. How can you provide easier texts for them or build extra reading support into their instructional days? What small-group instruction might benefit them? Moreover, consider how you can share information about reading with students and their parents. Knowing that they are making progress will keep students engaged in their learning. Assessment conversations are also good ways to help students develop more abstract concepts about reading. And parents, of course, are both interested in their children's progress in school and frequently willing to assist in their children's education. Tierney (1998) reminds us that it's important to keep parents not only informed but also involved: "Rather than keep the parent or caregiver at arm's length . . . , we need to embrace the concerns that parents have and the contributions they can make" (p. 380).

Evaluate Your Current Assessment Practices

The chart that follows may help you take a careful look at your current assessment practices in reading for all students, the students in Tier 1. To complete the chart, first list all the ways you currently assess students' reading in the "Assessment Tool/ Strategy" column. Then consider the information that each tool or strategy provides about each of the critical aspects of reading and mark the chart accordingly: + = excellent source of information; − = some information; [blank] = no information. When the chart is complete, make plans for assessment revision by asking the following questions:

- Are some critical aspects receiving too much/not enough attention?
- Can some tools/strategies be eliminated or revised?
- Do the assessments provide information about which students will need more targeted instruction in Tier 2?
- What revisions will enhance your overall assessment strategies?

Critical Aspects:
Reading Elements Assessment

Assessment Tool/Strategy	Phonemic Awareness	Phonics	Fluency	Vocabulary	Comprehension

Notes about revisions:

_____

_____

_____

_____

Ideas for Assessment

What did you conclude by analyzing your current strategies for assessing reading? Perhaps you are satisfied that you have enough of the right kind of information about your students. If not, you may find some of the following ideas helpful for supplementing your plans. As you consider the following ideas, take particular note of those that could supplement your current plans to identify and monitor those students who need more-targeted Tier 2 instruction. (*Note:* The other books in this series offer additional assessment options for phonemic awareness [Mraz, Padak, & Rasinski, 2008], phonics/decoding [Zimmerman, Padak, & Rasinski, 2008], fluency [Padak & Rasinski, 2008], vocabulary [Newton, Padak, & Rasinski, 2008], and comprehension [Rasinski & Padak, 2008a].)

Phonemic Awareness

This observation chart can be useful at those times when children show their phonemic awareness abilities. It is also useful in identifying and monitoring progress for students who need more-targeted instruction in Tier 2.

You can make brief notes on the chart or use some kind of symbol system, such as O = Outstanding, S = Satisfactory, and U = Unsatisfactory. Since assessing your children in Tier 1 in this way once every month or two may provide enough information to guide instruction, you can focus on different students each week and, over time, observe all your students. This way you can also focus on assessing your special needs students more often than the students in Tier 1—say, every other week or monthly.

Observation Chart

Aspect	Child's Name	Child's Name	Child's Name	Child's Name
Rhyming				
Phoneme Identity				
Blending/ Segmenting				
Deleting/ Substituting				

Phoneme isolation, identification, and blending can be assessed with Rasinski and Padak's (2008b) adaptation of the *Yopp–Singer Test of Phonemic Segmentation* (Yopp, 1995), shown in Figure 2.2.

This test is a set of 22 words that students segment into constituent sounds. For example, when you present the word *dog* orally, the appropriate response is for the child to say the three separate sounds that make up *dog*: /d/ /o/ /g/. We expect any students at second grade or beyond to score a 20 or more on this assessment. For students who score lower, you can graph the progress made on the test to monitor your targeted interventions for phonemic awareness.

Test of Phonemic Segmentation

Student's name _____ Date _____

Student's age _____

Score (number correct) _____ Examiner _____

Directions: I'd like to play a sound game with you. I will say a word and I want you to break the word apart into its sounds. You need to tell me each sound in the word. For example, if I say "old," you should say "/o/-/l/-/d/." (*Administrator: Be sure to say the sounds in the word distinctly. Do not say the letters.*) Let's try a few practice words.

Practice items: (Assist the child in segmenting these items as necessary. You may wish to use blocks to help demonstrate the segmentation of sounds.) kite, so, fat

Test items: (Circle those items that the student correctly segments; incorrect responses may be recorded on the blank line following the item.)

1. to _____	12. dock _____
2. me _____	13. lace _____
3. fight _____	14. mop _____
4. low _____	15. this _____
5. he _____	16. jot _____
6. vain _____	17. grow _____
7. is _____	18. nice _____
8. am _____	19. cat _____
9. be _____	20. shoe _____
10. meet _____	21. bed _____
11. jack _____	22. stay _____

Figure 2.2 Test for Assessing Phonemic Awareness

Source: Rasinski & Padak, *From Phonics to Fluency*, Figure 4.1 "Test for Assessing Phonemic Awareness," p. 46, © 2008. Reproduced by permission of Pearson Education, Inc.

Phonics

This observation chart is useful at those times when children show their phonics abilities. It is also useful in identifying and monitoring progress for students who need more-targeted Tier 2 instruction.

As with the phonemic awareness observation chart, you can make brief notes on the chart or use some kind of symbol system, such as O = Outstanding, S = Satisfactory, and U = Unsatisfactory. Since assessing your children in Tier 1 in this way once every month or two may provide enough information to guide instruction, you can focus on different students each week and, over time, observe all your students. This way you can also focus on assessing your special needs students more often than the students in Tier 2—say, every other week or monthly.

Observation Chart

Aspect	Child's Name	Child's Name	Child's Name	Child's Name
Awareness of Difficulty				
Knowledge of Letter–Sound Correspondences				
Skill in Applying Phonics Knowledge				
Ability to Check for Meaning				

Because phonics instruction should include a focus on onsets and rimes, it makes sense to use an assessment of common rimes. Rimes (or phonograms or word families) are the parts of words that contain the vowel and the letters that follow. The following chart includes common rimes along with one-syllable and multisyllable words containing them (adapted from Rasinski & Padak, 2008b, p. 265).

Rime	1-syllable	Multisyllable	Notes
-ay	Say	Playmate	
-ill	Spill	Willful	
-ip	Ship	Skipping	
-at	Bat	Satisfy	
-am	Slam	Hamster	
-ag	Brag	Shaggy	
-ack	Stack	Packer	
-ank	Crank	Blanket	
-ick	Quick	Cricket	
-ell	Yell	Shellfish	
-ot	Got	Hotcake	
-ing	King	Stacking	
-ap	Clap	Kidnap	
-unk	Junk	Bunker	
-ail	Nail	Railroad	
-ain	Chain	Mainstay	
-eed	Weed	Seedling	
-y	Try	Myself	
-out	Spout	Without	
-ug	Bug	Dugout	
-op	Stop	Popcorn	
-in	Chin	Tinsel	
-an	Stan	Flannel	

Rime	1-syllable	Multisyllable	Notes
-est	Nest	Chester	
-ink	Think	Trinket	
-ow	Grow	Snowball	
-ew	Chew	Newest	
-ore	Score	Adore	
-ed	Red	Bedtime	
-ab	Crab	Dabble	
-ob	Knob	Robber	
-ock	Block	Jockey	
-ake	Brake	Remake	
-ine	Shine	Porcupine	
-ight	Light	Sighted	
-im	Brim	Swimming	
-uck	Stuck	Truckload	
-um	Chum	Drummer	

You can ask children to read the words in lists or on cards, or you can put them into simple sentences (e.g., for –ay: Say "you will be my playmate") for the children to read. Make note of errors or patterns of error that occur, and use this information to help you decide what each child needs to learn next. You can also plot the numbers of one-syllable and multisyllable words pronounced correctly on a graph to monitor the children's progress on rimes.

The *Names Test*, which follows, can be used to create a baseline and progress graph for a variety of phonics elements. These elements include initial consonants, initial consonant blends, consonant digraphs, short vowels, long vowels, vowel digraphs, controlled vowels, and the schwa. The *Names Test* shows 70 words (names) and the scoring matrix you can use after you mark each child's errors while reading aloud.

Table 3
Protocol Sheet for the Names Test

Name _____ Grade _____ Teacher _____ Date _____

Jay Conway	Tim Cornell	Chuck Hoke	Yolanda Clark
Kimberly Blake	Roberta Slade	Homer Preston	Gus Quincy
Cindy Sampson	Chester Wright	Ginger Yale	Patrick Tweed
Stanley Shaw	Wendy Swain	Glen Spencer	Fred Sherwood
Flo Thornton	Dee Skidmore	Grace Brewster	Ned Westmoreland
Ron Smitherman	Troy Whitlock	Vance Middleton	Zane Anderson
Bernard Pendergraph	Shane Fletcher	Floyd Sheldon	Dean Bateman
Austin Shepherd	Bertha Dale	Neal Wade	Jake Murphy
Joan Brooks	Gene Loomis	Thelma Rinehart	

Phonics category	Errors
Initial consonants	___/37
Initial consonant blends	___/19
Consonant digraphs	___/15
Short vowels	___/36
Long vowels/VC-final e	___/23
Vowel digraphs	___/15
Controlled vowels	___/25
Schwa	___/15

Table 4
Scoring Matrix for the Names Test

Name _____ Date _____

Name	InCon	InConBl	ConDgr	ShVow	LngVow/VC-e	VowDgr	CtrVow	Schwa
Anderson				A			er	o
Austin						Au		i
Bateman	B				ate			a
Bernard	B						er, ar	
Bertha	B		th				er	a
Blake		Bl			ake			
Brewster		Br					ew, er	
Brooks		Br				oo		
Chester			Ch	e			er	
Chuck			Ch	u				
Cindy	C			i		y		
Clark		Cl					ar	
Conway	C			o		ay		
Cornell	C			e			or	
Dale	D				ale			
Dean	D					ea		
Dee	D					ee		
Fletcher		Fl	ch	e			er	
Flo		Fl			o			
Floyd		Fl				oy		
Fred		Fr		e				
Gene	G				ene			

(continued)

Table 4
Scoring Matrix for the Names Test (cont'd.)

Name	InCon	InConBl	ConDgr	ShVow	LngVow/VC-e	VowDgr	CtrVow	Schwa
Ginger	G			i			er	
Glen		Gl		e				
Grace		Gr			ace			
Gus	G			u				
Hoke	H				oke			
Homer	H				o		er	
Jake	J				ake			
Jay	J					ay		
Joan	J					oa		
Kimberly	K			i	y		er	
Loomis	L					oo		i
Middleton	M			i				o
Murphy	M		ph		y		ur	
Neal	N					ea		
Ned	N			e				
Patrick	P			a, i				
Pendergraph	P		ph	e, a			er	
Preston		pr		e				o
Quincy				i	y			
Rinehart	R				ine		ar	
Roberta	R				o		er	a
Ron	R			o				
Sampson	S			a				o
Shane			Sh		ane			
Shaw			Sh				aw	
Sheldon			Sh	e				o

Name	InCon	InConBl	ConDgr	ShVow	LngVow/VC-e	VowDgr	CtrVow	Schwa
Shepherd			Sh	e			er	
Sherwood			Sh			oo	er	
Skidmore		Sk		i			or	
Slade		Sl			ade			
Smitherman		Sm	th	i			er	a
Spencer		Sp		e			er	
Stanley		St		a		ey		
Swain		Sw				ai		
Thelma			Th	e				a
Thornton			Th				or	o
Tim	T			i				
Troy		Tr				oy		
Tweed		Tw				ee		
Vance	V			a				
Wade	W				ade			
Wendy	W			e	y			
Westmoreland	W			e			or	a
Whitlock			Wh	i, o				
Wright					i			
Yale	Y				ale			
Yolanda	Y			a	o			a
Zane	Z				ane			

Source: Tables 3 and 4 from Duffelmeyer, F. A., Kruse, A. E., Merkley, D. J., & Fyfe, S. A. (October, 1994). Further validation and enhancement of the Names Test. *The Reading Teacher, 48*(2), 118–129. Reprinted with permission of the International Reading Association.

Fluency

This observation chart can be useful at those times when students show their fluency abilities. It is also useful in identifying and monitoring progress for students who need more-targeted Tier 2 instruction.

As with the previous observation charts, you can make brief notes on the chart or use some kind of symbol system, such as O = Outstanding, S = Satisfactory, and U = Unsatisfactory. Since assessing your children in Tier 1 in this way once every month or two may provide enough information to guide instruction, you can focus on different students each week and, over time, observe all students. This way you can also focus on assessing students with special needs more often than the students in Tier 1—say, every other week or monthly.

Observation Chart

Aspect	Child's Name	Child's Name	Child's Name	Child's Name
Rate				
Accuracy				
Expression				
Volume and Clarity				
Eye Contact/ Gestures				

The *Oral Reading Fluency Scale* is a valuable tool to monitor the progress of Tier 2 students at multiple points in time. You can listen to children read and rate their performance against research-based standards. This rubric was developed as part of a federal research project to ascertain the fluency of U.S. fourth graders (Pinnell et al., 1995). We have adapted it for your use:

5 Outstanding	Appropriate phrasing. Regressions or repetitions, if any, do not detract from presentation. Expressive. Appropriate rate. Few hesitations or stops.
4 Satisfactory	Mostly appropriate phrasing. Expressive interpretation inconsistent. Rate generally appropriate. Occasional hesitations or stops.
3 Unsatisfactory	Reads in short inappropriate phrases. Little expressive interpretation. Rate inappropriately slow. Extended hesitations and stops.
2 Unsatisfactory	Word-by-word reading. Very little/no expression or interpretation. Few word recognition errors. Excessively slow (or fast) rate.
1 Unsatisfactory	Excessive word recognition errors significantly disrupt fluency and meaning.

Fluency progress of students with special needs in fluency can also be graphed at multiple points in time using the *Oral Reading Rate Norms*. Although fluency is more than reading quickly, comparing students' rates of reading against established norms can provide helpful information. To do this, simply ask a student to read aloud for one minute. Make note of how many words the child reads correctly and compare the total to the following chart (adapted from Hasbrouck & Tindal, 1992; Howe & Shin, 2001; and Rasinski & Padak, 2005a, 2005b). Students whose rates fall near these norms should be considered as making satisfactory progress in fluency. Students whose rates are substantially below these norms have fluency problems. Those whose rates are substantially above these norms deserve further consideration. A very rapid reading rate may also be indicative of fluency problems if the listener's understanding is impeded.

Grade	Fall	Winter	Spring
1	0–20	20–40	40–60
2	40–60	50–80	70–100
3	60–90	70–100	90–120
4	90–110	100–120	110–130
5	95–115	110–130	120–140
6	105–125	120–140	135–155

Vocabulary

This observation chart can be useful at times when students show their vocabulary abilities. It is also useful in identifying and monitoring progress for students who need more-targeted Tier 2 instruction.

As with the previous observation charts, you can make brief notes on the chart or use some kind of symbol system, such as O = Outstanding, S = Satisfactory, and U = Unsatisfactory. Since assessing students in Tier 1 in this way once every month or two may

Observation Chart

Indicator	Child's Name	Child's Name	Child's Name	Child's Name
Decodes words already in meaning vocabulary				
Learns new concepts (or labels for concepts)				
Uses new vocabulary orally and in writing				
Applies strategies to learn new words (structure, semantics, metacognition)				
Uses reference works and other resources to learn new words				

provide enough information to guide instruction, you can focus on different students each week and, over time, observe all your students. This way you can also focus on assessing your special needs students more often than the students in Tier 1—say, every other week or monthly.

Many instructional activities have vocabulary assessment value. In Newton et al. (2008), we list several that work particularly well: List–Group–Label, Word Sorts, Important Words, Wide Reading, Expressing Thoughts, Sentence Starters, Words Knew and New, Odd Word Out, Matching, Multiple Choice Cloze, One-Minute Meetings, and several self-assessments. Although no single occasion will provide a complete picture of a student's vocabulary knowledge and ability, notes about performance with these may be useful. You might want to create a chart with students' names down one side and activities/dates across the top; you can then use the O–S–U notation system to summarize children's performance. This chart can be used to record additional vocabulary information for Tier 1 students and/or to monitor progress for Tier 2 students.

In using these strategies, select words that the class or a particular student has generated for a word wall or collected on cards as new sight words or interesting words from readings. Using words from prior instruction makes the assessment authentic and allows for comparisons of vocabulary growth at multiple points in time.

Observation Chart

Aspect	Child's Name	Child's Name	Child's Name	Child's Name
Concepts				
Word Roots				
Context Clues				
Discussion				
Composition				
Word Exploration				

With these words, you can simply have the student keep track of known words on a chart. Or you can use a word sort to evaluate how the student understands, associates, and uses the words. You can create a chart with the words and space for notes to record progress in these areas:

Word	Understands Word	Associates Word	Uses/Applies Word

A *Knowledge Rating Chart* (Blachowicz & Fisher, 2006) can also assist in monitoring vocabulary progress. The following chart has a place for words down the side and three columns for the student to rate word knowledge: (a) know the word well, (b) have seen/heard the word, and (c) don't know the word at all. You can use words from prior instruction as a formative assessment of what words the student has or has not come to know. Or you can use the chart before and after instruction to assess what the student learned. Overall, these charts can keep track of the words learned, while also informing continued vocabulary instruction.

Word	Know the word well	Have seen/heard the word	Don't know the word at all

Comprehension

This observation chart can be useful at those times when children show their comprehension abilities. It is also useful in identifying and monitoring progress for students who need more-targeted instruction in Tier 2.

As with the previous observation charts, you can make brief notes on the chart or use some kind of symbol system, such as O = Outstanding, S = Satisfactory, and U = Unsatisfactory. Because assessing students in Tier 1 in this way once every month or two may provide enough information to guide instruction, you can focus on different students each week and, over time, observe all your students. This way you can also focus on assessing students with special needs more often than the students in Tier 1—say, every other week or monthly.

Observation Chart

Aspect	Child's Name	Child's Name	Child's Name	Child's Name
Retelling/Summarizing				
Going Beyond Literal Text Meaning				
Exhibiting Critical Understanding and Text Judgment				
Monitoring Comprehension				

Observational progress notes for comprehension strategy use, retelling, and self-assessment are also useful assessment tools for Tier 2 students. Specifically, the progress notes show how often students are using strategies for comprehension, such as developing background knowledge, using imagery, or making connections. Retellings provide information about the extent to which students are gaining information when they read a text. Self-assessments foster students' sense of responsibility alongside self-monitoring of their comprehension. You can use these assessments more often or in more depth to look at struggling readers' comprehension abilities and to monitor their progress.

To observe progress on comprehension strategy use, create a chart that lists the strategies that you used in your targeted instruction. Then create columns that indicate multiple points in time (e.g., each month) where you indicate whether or not the child uses the strategy. Leave space for notes about your conclusions as well. This progress chart will provide information about what the student has learned and what he or she still needs in terms of targeted comprehension instruction.

A retelling, on the other hand, provides you with a method for assessing the whole of comprehension. It answers the question, To what extent are students gaining meaning from what they read? To conduct a retelling, you ask students to read a passage either orally or silently, and after reading, you ask them to retell or tell you what they remember from the reading. Then you judge the quality of their retelling against a descriptive rubric. Following are some things to keep in mind when using a retelling procedure to assess comprehension:

- Tell students before they read the text that you will be asking them to recall or tell you what they remember from the reading when they are finished.

- When students finish reading the passage, give them a few seconds to collect their thoughts, remove the text from their view, and ask them to tell you all they can remember from the reading.

- Feel free to prompt students to recall more information when they end their recall or tell you that there is nothing more they can remember. You might ask, "Is there anything else you remember from the passage?" and give them a few seconds to recall. You might ask students to give their opinion about the text or any element within it. Or you might ask if reading the text made them think about or connect with anything from their own experiences. The last two prompts allow students to go beyond the text and provide inferences that they might not spontaneously provide.

The following rubric allows you to judge the quality of the retelling. As you can see, it ranges from a score of 1 for a minimal recall to a score of 6, which reflects a comprehensive, logical summary that also goes beyond the text into logical inferences the student might make about the content.

Informal Retelling Comprehension Assessment

Ask the reader to retell what he or she can remember after having read a text. Score the student's comments against the following rubric (adapted from Rasinski & Padak, 2005a, 2005b).

1. Recalls a fact or two minimally, if at all. Facts recalled may or may not be important.
2. Recalls a number of unrelated facts of varied importance.
3. Recalls the main idea of the passage with a few supporting details.
4. Recalls the main idea along with a fairly robust set of supporting details.
5. Provides a comprehensive summary of the passage, logically developed and elaborate; includes a statement of the main idea.
6. Provides a comprehensive summary and makes inferences that go beyond the text. The inferences may be in the form of connections to the student's own life, reasonable judgments about the text or characters or items within the text, or logical predictions about events that go beyond the boundaries of the text itself.

To monitor progress in comprehension, administer retelling assessments often, graph the results, and use the results to decide how the student is responding to the targeted comprehension instruction. Also, during a retelling assessment, notice whether poor comprehension is due to other factors such as problems with word recognition or fluency. To control for such factors and to help you decide if problems are related more to fluency or decoding than to comprehension, you may wish to have students retell material that you read to them. When the word recognition and fluency load is removed by your reading the text to students, are they able to provide an adequate retelling of the passage? A comparison of students' retellings when they read the text and when the text is read to them may give you good information about the extent to which other factors may influence and perhaps inhibit students' understanding of what they read.

Self-assessment is another progress-monitoring tool to consider. You could engage students in conversations aimed at helping them think about their own comprehension abilities and progress. Questions like these may help you help students think about their growth as readers:

- Think back to [some time earlier—say, a month before the conversation]. Is it easier for you to understand what you read now than it was then? How do you know?

- When you read, what are you good at? What parts of reading give you trouble?

- What do you do if you can't understand what you are reading? How does this strategy work for you?

Progress Monitoring for All Students

The assessment tools described in this chapter can help you gather focused information about students who have special needs in reading. In particular, you can learn about students' phonemic awareness, phonics/decoding capabilities, fluency, vocabulary and comprehension abilities. Giving these assessments periodically and summarizing results for individual readers and across all students in your classroom will allow you to monitor students' progress, which in turn can help you make effective instructional decisions.

However, reading is also influenced by factors such as background knowledge, perceived purpose, instructional expectations, and type of materials or activities. These factors vary among students, but even for an individual, they may vary throughout the school day or from one day to the next. Thus, your plan for monitoring students' progress in reading must be broader than the assessments summarized earlier in the chapter. Observations and conversations with students can provide you with the additional information you need to complete your portraits of students as readers.

Daily opportunities to observe readers "in action" are abundant. Select one student with special needs in reading to observe every day. Watch this child for a minute or two in a variety of reading and reading-related situations. What happens during teacher read-aloud? Independent reading? Free-choice time? Instruction in reading? Instruction in content areas? What happens when the child works independently? With peers? In teacher-directed situations?

Keep notes about what you observe, and look for patterns of behavior. When, in general, is the student successful? Unsuccessful or frustrated? Recurring behaviors are likely to be meaningful. Draw conclusions about how the student reads and responds to instruction. Add this information to the assessment results you have gathered.

Conversations with students can also provide helpful information for monitoring their progress in reading. By asking the right kinds of questions in the right ways and listening carefully to how students respond, you can learn about students' actions and attitudes as readers. These conversations can be informal, on-the-fly chats, or more formal, as when they are part of planned reading conferences. Make notes about conversations, and add this information to other assessment information you have about your students.

Observational data and notes about conversations can help you understand not just how a child is reading but also perhaps why he or she is reading in this way. And answers to both these questions—the how and the why—provide a useful platform for understanding the results of other assessments.

Assessment should enable you to determine how students with special needs are responding to targeted instruction in phonemic awareness, phonics, fluency, vocabulary, and comprehension. Some students may need targeted instruction for all of the reading elements, while others may move between Tier 1 and Tier 2 in particular reading elements, depending on their progress.

In order to monitor all students' progress, consider using a class summary chart like the following. In the first column, write the names of the students in your class. In the next five columns depicting the reading elements, use 1 or 2 to indicate which tier you use to plan instruction for that child. Summarize information from other assessments of the particular reading elements in the boxes as well. Use the last column for notes. For example, if you use a chart like this quarterly, use the "Comments" column to note the tier a student may have moved from or to between quarters or to identify any student that should be considered for Tier 3, the most intensive interventions.

Student Name	Phonemic Awareness	Phonics	Fluency	Vocabulary	Comprehension	Comments

After you have charted assessment information, you need to use it for instructional planning. This may involve looking for instructional groups: Which students could benefit from focused instruction in vocabulary or fluency, for example? It may also involve looking across an individual student's assessment information to hypothesize about how the various pieces of his or her reading performance may be related. Suppose Alicia and Bob have equally weak comprehension scores, but Alicia reads very quickly (too quickly, even), while Bob does not. Or suppose Carlos and Diane also have equally weak comprehension scores, but Carlos has serious decoding difficulties, but Diane does not. Instructionally, Bob and Diane need to focus on comprehension, Alicia needs to learn to slow down and focus on meaning, and Carlos needs to have decoding instruction.

Monitoring students' reading and making wise instructional decisions involve more than simply giving assessments. They also involve combining your concrete knowledge about the classroom and particular students with your theoretical knowledge about how students learn, what reading is, and how readers develop.

Plans for Change

In this chapter, you have evaluated your own assessment strategies for reading and, as a result, perhaps generated some ideas for change. Use the following chart to make notes about the changes you want to make. As you do so, make sure that these changes reflect the "big ideas" we outlined at the beginning of the chapter:

- Focus on critical information.
- Look for patterns of behavior.
- Recognize children's developmental progressions (can't, can sometimes, can always) and cultural or linguistic differences.
- Be parsimonious when gathering assessment information.
- Use instructional situations for assessment purposes.

You may want to share your plans with others to get their feedback.

Goal Planning: Reading Assessment

Goal _____

Plans by _____ Date _____

Action Steps: What do I need to do?	Materials: What resources do I need?	Evaluation: How will I assess the usefulness of this change?

Professional Development Suggestions

Book Club

Develop Instructional Recommendations

Work with colleagues to make instructional recommendations for these third graders. Talk through the rationale for your decisions. (O = Outstanding, S = Satisfactory, and U = Unsatisfactory.)

Student	Decoding	Fluency	Vocabulary	Comprehension
Daniel	O	U	S	U
Jourdan	O	S	S	U
Malina	S	S	S	S
Terek	S	U	U	U

- Instructional plans for Daniel: _____

  _____

  _____

  Rationale: _____

  _____

- Instructional plans for Jourdan: _____

  _____

  _____

  Rationale: _____

  _____

- Instructional plans for Malina: _____

  _____

  _____

  Rationale: _____

  _____

- Instructional plans for Terek: _____

_____

_____

Rationale: _____

_____

Instructional Strategies for Teaching Learners with Special Needs

Guiding Principles for Instruction

After years of teaching kindergarten and the primary grades, Ms. Fernandez expects a wide range of developmental levels and literacy foundations among young students. Some children enter school from literacy-rich home environments where they've been immersed in language and books. They have an interest in books and even have favorite books or stories. They also recognize common words, understand letter–sound relationships, and know the names of things. They will recognize, for example, the word *man* and be able to say the sounds in the word (/m/ /a/ /n/) and then point to a picture that the word represents.

Others arrive in Ms. Fernandez's classroom from homes where literacy has not been emphasized, and their exposure to words and books has been limited. They do not identify favorite books. They also have difficulty with identifying common words, understanding letter–sound relationships, and knowing the names of things. In addition, a growing number of kindergarten and primary-level children have native languages other than English. For all these reasons, Ms. Fernandez knows that she needs differentiated plans for reading instruction for these students who have special reading needs.

Mr. Washington teaches fifth grade in the same school. He, too, expects students to vary in terms of their reading abilities and needs. Some of his students have been avid readers for years. They have favorite authors and are eager to share what they're reading independently. They are equally comfortable reading fiction and informational texts and read their content area materials successfully. He believes these students are well on their way to developing into lifelong readers.

Some of Mr. Washington's students struggle with reading, and he has noticed that their needs vary. Many are fairly good decoders; they can say the words in texts they read. Comprehension, however, is another story. It seems as if these students are focusing so much on saying words that they're not even thinking about the author's message as they read. These difficulties are exacerbated when students work with content area materials. Comprehending science and social studies texts seems beyond many students' capabilities. Some read in a slow and labored way, which suggests fluency problems that Mr. Washington thinks may be related to decoding and comprehension difficulties. Unfortunately, students with these reading struggles are developing negative attitudes about reading and themselves as readers. Mr. Washington fears that they may be giving up.

In order to provide instruction that supports students with special needs in their classrooms, both Ms. Fernandez and Mr. Washington first decide on a number of instructional routines. Ms. Fernandez focuses instruction on all five elements of reading, while Mr. Washington decides to focus on just three—fluency, vocabulary, and comprehension. In evaluating possible routines for use in their classrooms, both teachers think about the extent to which the routines reflect important instructional principles for students with special needs in the regular classroom:

1. Students need *systematic instruction* in the essential components of reading. Systematic instruction is planned, sequential, and based on goals for particular students as readers. Both teachers will determine what struggling readers know and can do, decide on what assistance they need, select strategies to implement, draw conclusions about the outcomes of instruction, and decide what to revise.

2. Students need *social interaction* while making progress in reading. This can come in the form of peer interaction, where peers have opportunities to talk through reading, or in individual instruction, where the student has opportunities to talk through the process. When working together, students perform at a slightly higher cognitive level because talking helps them to enhance their thinking and to incorporate the talk of others to solve problems (Vygotsky, 1978). One important way to enhance the cognitive level and the talking-through process is to have a peer or adult work as the scribe while the student with special needs talks through the process.

3. Students need to develop *skills in self-regulating* their reading. They need to become metacognitive, to learn how to think through their thinking, to monitor their success in reading, and to apply "fix-up" strategies when needed.

4. Teaching is the process of making visible that which is often invisible to students. Students need *concrete visual scaffolds* associated with their reading strategies. They benefit from a strategy they can see while learning because they can weave together the information that they visualize (Clark & Pavio, 1991). Graphic organizers are wonderful concrete visual scaffolds; for example, imagine a graphic that depicts the initial event, the rising action, the conflict, the falling action, and the ending of a story (as shown in Figure 3.1). Students can use the graphic, either independently or with assistance, to make notes about important information while reading or listening to a story.

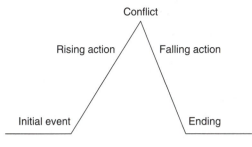

Figure 3.1 Plot Map

51
....

CHAPTER 3

*Instructional
Strategies for
Teaching Learners
with Special Needs*

Professional Development Suggestions

Evaluating Your Own Instruction

Before adding new strategies and activities to your instructional repertoire, it is important to evaluate your current teaching practices for students with special needs in various elements of reading: What current instructional practices do you find to be effective? What instructional areas need to be fine-tuned? Are there instructional components that are not being addressed to the degree that they need to be?

To help you in evaluating your status quo, consider the following semantic feature analysis chart.. Along the side of the chart, you will see space for you to list those instructional strategies that you currently use to enhance students' literacy learning. You can key the strategies to particular emphases: PA = phonemic awareness, P = phonics/decoding, F = fluency, V = vocabulary, and C = comprehension. Across the top of the chart, you will see components that may be present in the activities that you listed. Of course, not every component can, or should, be part of every activity. Some activities will encourage students to interact with classmates, for example; others may invite a more independent response. The key is to seek a balance in terms of the variety of strategies used so that a range of developmental levels and diverse learner needs can be effectively addressed.

Take the time to complete the semantic feature analysis. Place a + sign in the corresponding box for each attribute that is present in a literacy instructional activity that you currently use. More than one attribute may be present for each activity that you list. In addition, you may wish to note strategies that could easily be altered to incorporate the kind of support that struggling readers need. You

52
....

CHAPTER 3

Instructional
Strategies for
Teaching Learners
with Special Needs

may wish to collaborate with colleagues; others may help you recall additional strategies that you use during the course of the school year.

When the semantic feature analysis is complete, it should help you analyze learning opportunities for students with special needs in reading. Which aspects of reading instruction currently receive a great deal of attention in your classroom? Which aspects need additional (or different) emphasis? Knowing this will help you to better plan adjustments in your instructional routine. Discuss your findings and insights with colleagues.

Semantic Feature Analysis for Current Instructional Practices for Students with Special Needs

Instructional Strategy*	Systematic Instruction	Social Interaction	Self-Monitoring	Concrete Visual Scaffolds

*For the instructional strategy, include the elements addressed: PA, P, F, V, and/or C.

Instructional Planning: Some Guidelines

The bulk of this chapter describes ways to alter instruction to meet the needs of Tier 2 students in your classroom. We would be remiss, however, if we didn't begin by commenting on some broad organizing principles for instruction. These apply to all your students—but perhaps especially to students with special needs in reading. Why? A significant number of research studies, spanning more than 20 years, have shown that the traditional skill-and-drill instruction doesn't work for Tier 2 students. Moreover, students who receive such instruction rarely, if ever, improve sufficiently to rejoin their Tier 1 peers (Allington, 1987, 2000, 2002; Allington & McGill-Franzen, 1989; Allington, Stuetzel, Shake, & Lamarche, 1986; Allington & Walmsley, 1995). Instead, students who receive this isolated skill instruction tend to remain behind classmates who achieve at more normal rates. Sadly, they begin to see themselves as failures and to view reading as a meaningless and frustrating task—as something to be avoided. Allington and others say that it is time to reinvent "remedial" reading.

We agree and believe that this reinvention should begin with attention to the principles of Response to Intervention (RTI) described earlier in this book. In addition, we hope you will use the following four principles as you plan instruction.

Provide Authentic and Engaging Reading Experiences

Do your best to ensure that what students read, how they read it, and how they respond to what they read (and write) connect to their interests and their lives. Plan reading tasks that students will approach eagerly—with curiosity, thoughtfulness, and an "I can do this" attitude. Consider the value of your own read-aloud sessions as well.

Motivation and interest are best fostered when students care about their reading. Encourage students to select their own reading material. Invite them to react, ask questions, and seek answers. In this way, you can help students learn to control the purpose, content, and direction of their reading experiences.

Maximize Time for "Eyes on Print"

Becoming a reader depends in part on opportunities to read. Research from the last 20 years has consistently shown that students who read more at school and at home achieve more in reading than do their peers who do not (e.g., National Assessment of Educational Progress 1992, 1994, 1998, 2000 [U.S. Department of Education, 2001]; Progress in International Reading Literacy Study 2001, 2006 [Martin, Mullis, & Kennedy, 2007]). Furthermore, Krashen (2004), a noted researcher on English language learners, maintains that free voluntary reading enhances language acquisition for these students.

To give your students opportunities to become readers, you can do two things. First, provide them with ample time to practice reading—to read—each day. Second, provide access to authentic material that students find interesting and easy to read. Both these choices are associated with highly effective teachers (Allington, 2002).

Provide Support When Needed

Students with special needs in reading often struggle to read material that others find far less daunting. You must be ready and able to provide support (or scaffolding) to make each reading experience meaningful and successful. No reader should ever struggle to the point of failure or frustration.

Support can take a variety of forms. You may want to read a text to or with students before asking them to read it on their own, a choice that may be especially good if you are required to use material that is too challenging for your Tier 2 students. Peer activities, such as buddy, paired, or echo reading, can be useful as well.

Instruction in specific skills or strategies can also provide support. Provide this instruction as needed—that is, only if you see that lack of a particular strategy or bit of reading knowledge is hampering a student's progress. Make no assumptions about student need; rather, take your cues from student performance (Rasinski, Padak, & Fawcett, 2010).

Be Consistent Over Time

A consistent instructional routine that includes authentic reading experiences as well as instructional activity in the area of difficulty makes lessons predictable for students and for you. This predictability leads to student independence, more efficient use of time, and greater on-task behavior. Consistent routines need not be boring. Vary instructional activities within the general framework of your reading curriculum. Who will read? How? How will students respond to what they have read? These questions and more can help you develop lively, interesting instruction that will foster students' growth as readers and offer them authentic, engaging reading experiences.

To develop this consistent routine, first think about the time available for reading and reading-related activities. Ideally, devote two hours each day to reading (Allington, 2002). Now break this large amount of time into chunks: How much time will you devote to read-aloud each day? To students' independent reading? Will you provide whole-group instruction? Small-group instruction? If the latter, what will the rest of the class do while you are working with a small group? To double-check your decisions, think about your instructional goals: Are you providing students daily opportunities to achieve these goals?

Instructional planning is part of your professional responsibility. As Pressley (2002) has noted, "There are no quick fixes with regard to improving children's literacy. There's no reform package that a school can buy that delivers improved achievement with certainty. The influences of packaged reforms are often uneven or small" (p. 180). Packaged reforms don't work. Your careful planning and delivery of needs-based instruction does.

Strategy Suggestions

Researchers have categorized strategies for students with special needs as those that are student-mediated, teacher-mediated, or peer-mediated (e.g., Reid & Lienemann, 2006; Ryan, Reid, & Epstein, 2004). Student-mediated strategies generally focus on self-monitoring, like completing a checklist for the parts of a book read or filling in a character map while reading independently. Peer-mediated strategies are those for which two or more peers have cooperative responsibility, like counting the number of words a peer reads correctly or reading parts of a book and teaching each other about the text. Teacher-mediated strategies are those for which the teacher has responsibility, like praising a student or modifying the number of unknown vocabulary words to find in a given text.

Of these three, both student-mediated and peer-mediated strategies have long been shown to result in significant gains for students with special needs (Hoff & Robinson, 2002). Therefore, the strategies described in this chapter are ones that attend to the student's self-monitoring either individually or within a small group and that are facilitated by an adult. That adult can be a teacher, paraprofessional, or volunteer.

Most research-based strategies for the essential reading components can be adapted to work with students with special needs in

56
....
CHAPTER 3

*Instructional
Strategies for
Teaching Learners
with Special Needs*

reading. In this section, we describe several research-based strategies and explain adaptations that work particularly well for Tier 2 students. All of the strategies can be used one-on-one and in small groups and can be models for your own strategy adaptations for students with special needs. In addition, each adaptation reflects one or more of the four principles for teaching students with special needs: provide systematic instruction, encourage social interaction, teach self-regulation, and use concrete visual scaffolds. As you read descriptions of these adaptations, think about how you can adapt your current instruction to meet the needs of your Tier 2 students.

Phonemic Awareness: Sound Tasks

Background

When your instructional goal is to develop phonemic awareness, adapting these plans for Tier 2 students is easy. You can adapt the sound tasks strategy for students who are not accomplishing the desired phonemic awareness outcomes.

First, recall the definition of phonemic awareness: the ability to focus on and manipulate the spoken sounds of language in order to produce spoken words (Mraz, Padak, & Rasinski, 2008). A phoneme is the smallest unit of speech that affects the meaning of words. For example, the smallest units of speech in the word *cat* are /k/ /a/ /t/. The meaning of the word *cat* is affected when we replace the last phoneme, /t/, with the phoneme /b/. The word becomes *cab*, which is now a car that people pay to ride in rather than a domestic animal.

Like other phonemic awareness strategies (e.g., sound boxes, alliteration games), sound tasks should not be done all in one sitting. The National Reading Panel (2000) suggests engaging in phonemic awareness activities for five minutes a day and focusing on one sound task at a time.

A distinction between sound tasks for Tier 1 and Tier 2 students is the adaptation that includes the guiding principles of systematic instruction, social interaction, self-regulation, and concrete visual scaffolds. For Tier 2, you would select sound tasks as a strategy after analyzing both what the majority of the class can do and the abilities of your students who are struggling. As you will see, the tasks are extended with such adaptations as teacher prompts, images for visuals, self-monitoring such as pointing and checking off the accomplishment of each sound task, and peer interaction by having students talk through each sound and its related image together.

Purpose

To provide students with special needs individual and independent practice in the six sound tasks used in learning phonemic awareness.

Materials

The sound task chart, images provided here, and scissors if you choose to copy and cut the images in order to move them around on the chart while talking through each sound task. As the child improves,

Six Sound Tasks with Definitions, Teacher Prompts, and Correct Answers

Sound Task	Definition	Teacher Prompt	Correct Answer
Phoneme isolation	Child can recognize the first sound in words.	"Point to the picture of the cat. Tell me the first sound in *cat*."	/k/
Phoneme identity	Child can recognize a common sound in different words.	"Point to the pictures of the pan and the pig. Tell me the sound that is the same at the beginning of *pan* and *pig*."	/p/
Phoneme categorization	In a sequence of words, child can identify the odd sound.	"Point to the pictures of the pan, pig, and bug. Tell me the sound that does not belong in the following words: *pan, pig, bug*."	/b/ in bug: It has a different beginning sound. /n/ in pan: It has a different ending sound.
Phoneme blending	Child can identify spoken sounds and create a word.	"What word does /k/ /a/ /t/ create?"	Cat
Phoneme segmentation	Child can break a word into its individual sounds (e.g., by tapping).	"Point to the picture of the cat. How many sounds are in *cat*?"	Three (/k/ /a/ /t/)
Phoneme manipulation	Child can add, delete, or substitute sounds.	"Point to the pictures of the ramp, ball, and ram. What is the word *ramp* without /p/?" (deletion) "What is the word *ball* with /m/ instead of /b/?" (substitution) "What is the word *ram* when you add /p/ at the end?"	Ram Mall Ramp

Images Used for Sound Tasks (use this page in the book or copy and cut out the images)

you can print more images from programs such as Board Maker (a free trial is located at http://www.mayer-johnson.com) or from Internet searches such as Google Images (http://images.google.com).

Procedures

1. Select a student or group of students with needs in one area of phonemic awareness (see the following sound tasks chart). Prepare your images. Either use the page of this text with the images or copy the images to use them separately. Once copied, you can cut them and move them around while engaged in the individual sound tasks. You may even want to laminate the pictures for multiple use.

2. Read the teacher prompt for each sound task. If the child gets stuck on one sound task, first demonstrate the correct answer. Then use prompts that reflect other images provided.

3. Have the child point to images that you are using in the prompt in order to self-monitor, or indicate each sound task completed with a check mark or small item placed next to the images or sound task list.

Phonics: Onsets and Rimes

Background

Recall that, while phonemic awareness is about sounds, phonics is about letters and sounds. For example, given the spoken word *cat*, a child can say that it begins with the sound /k/ (phonemic awareness). Alternatively, while reading the word *cat*, a child can associate the letter "c" with the sound /k/.

When teaching onsets and rimes, adaptations for Tier 2 students should reflect the guiding principles of systematic instruction, social interaction, self-regulation, and concrete visual scaffolds. As you will see, instruction is extended with such adaptations as creating letter cards for decoding by analogy, creating word-family poems for concrete visual scaffolds, keeping track of known rimes as part of self-monitoring (in the last column of the self-monitoring chart that follows), and pairing with other students to select and explore chosen rimes.

Purpose

To provide students individual and social practice with onsets and the most common rimes in order to generate a large number of words.

Materials

The most common rimes table (see Appendix B), self-monitoring chart, and/or Venn diagram (Figure 3.2).

Procedures

1. Remind students that onsets are the consonants that precede the vowels in words and syllables (e.g., *s* in *sap*; *str* in *strap*).
2. Explain that rimes are vowels and the consonants that follow them in syllables (e.g., *op* in *mop*, *eet* in *street*).
3. Introduce a preselected number of rimes from the common rimes table (Appendix B). Provide examples of these rimes. If using the Three-Day or Five-Day Rime Time Routines (Zimmerman, Padak, & Rasinski, 2008), we recommend one rime per week for mid- to end-year kindergartners and first graders.

60
....

CHAPTER 3

*Instructional
Strategies for
Teaching Learners
with Special Needs*

4. Ask individual students to create a prespecified number of words containing each rimes (e.g., two).

5. Have students pair and create more words for each rime.

6. Repeat the task until teams create several words for each common rime. See the following variations and additions for using the chart.

Variations and Additions

1. Ask students to locate a prespecified number of rimes in a text you or they choose and fill in the third column of the self-monitoring chart with the words from the text.

2. Have students mark the last column of the chart. Perhaps they could use a check mark if they know the rime well and a question mark if they believe they need to revisit the rime for more practice.

3. Using the Venn diagram in Figure 3.2, have students compare and contrast

   a. Ending consonants of words with the same short vowel sound,

   b. Different short vowel rimes, or

   c. Rimes with the same written vowel symbol.

   For example, the word families *elt* and *ell* contain the same short vowel sound /e/. However, the ending consonants are different. Using the Venn diagram to show similarity and difference, the child could place the /e/ sound where the circles overlap, depicting /e/ as the similar sound in both rimes. Then the child could place *elt* and *ell* in the nonoverlapping parts of the circles to show that the ending consonants of the same short vowel sounds are different. You could extend this exercise with asking the child, "What words might we make out of these word families?"

4. Have students create letter cards for decoding by analogy. In decoding by analogy, children use rimes to infer the pronunciation of an unfamiliar word. For example, use letter cards, magnetic letters, or letter tiles to draw attention to the rime in a word they probably have not seen before, such as *ade* in

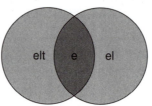

Figure 3.2   Venn Diagram Example

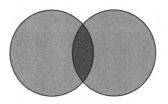

Figure 3.3 Blank Venn Diagram

shade. Then present *shade* next to a known word like *made.* Finally, replace the *m* in made with *sh* to make *shade.*

5. Use the chart while incorporating the Three-Day or the Five-Day Rime Time Routine.

6. Copy the self-monitoring chart for rime knowledge, and ask students to cut the words out. They can sort these into logical sets, such as those with the same short vowel sound, those with any short vowel sound, and so on.

Self-Monitoring Chart for Rime Knowledge

Rime	Word Example 1	Word Example 2	Example from Text	Know This Rime? (yes, ?)
-ing	Sing	King	King	yes

Fluency: Audio-Recorded Reading (Assisted Reading) and the Fluency Development Lesson

Background

When your instructional goal is to build fluency skills, adaptations from Tier 1 to Tier 2 easily fit with the instructional principles for students with special needs. Fluency is the ability to read expressively and meaningfully as well as accurately and with appropriate speed (Padak & Rasinski, 2008). Fluency builds a bridge between decoding with speed at the surface level and comprehension that can occur with successful surface-level decoding. Therefore, fluency is important because it influences comprehension.

Distinctions between audio-recorded or assisted reading for Tier 1 and Tier 2 students are found in the adaptations in systematic instruction, social interaction, self-regulation, and concrete visual scaffolds. Audio-recorded reading can be extended with such adaptations as using concrete visual organizers while following along (e.g., a character map [Figure 3.4] or a plot map [Figure 3.1]). Social interaction can be enhanced with peers comparing texts they read by sharing their maps. Social interaction is built into the Fluency Development Lesson, since students read texts to one another. Moreover, with either strategy, learners can also use simple checklists that you create, perhaps using smiley faces as response options. For audio-recorded reading, items on this checklist could include "I followed along for each paragraph," "I understood the selection," and "I completed as much of the selection as I planned." For the Fluency Development Lesson, students can rate themselves and/or their partners using items such as "The reading was smooth," "The reading sounded like talk," and "The reader's voice sounded good."

Audio-Recorded Reading

Purpose

To provide individual and independent practice in fluency.

Materials

Books with accompanying recordings. The recordings can be commercially produced, such as those that can be checked out from a library. Another alternative is to develop a classroom listening library by having students prepare audio-recorded versions of classroom books for their peers to use.

Procedures

63

CHAPTER 3

*Instructional
Strategies for
Teaching Learners
with Special Needs*

1. Create a listening center in the classroom. Headphones and audio recorders will work best. With many texts also on CD and audio files, CD players and older computers may also work well for this purpose.

2. Stock the listening center with engaging texts and corresponding CDs or other audio.

3. Provide students with 15–20 minutes per day at the listening center.

4. Help students select books that are (a) written at their instructional levels and (b) very likely to be engaging.

5. Remind students to follow along in the text as they listen to the audio recording.

6. Students may want to log the pages they read during each session with one of the following protocols.

Concrete visual scaffolds for audio-recorded reading can include graphic organizers or other charts that help with self-monitoring, comprehension, or vocabulary, such as the following protocols.

Audio-Recorded Reading 1

My book (copy the title): _____

Number of pages: _____

Pictures on the cover: _____

_____

_____

What I think will happen: _____

_____

_____

Turn on the recording. Listen and point to the words. Pause the recording after reading some pages (paused on page _____).

What happened? _____

_____

_____

Was my prediction right? _____

_____

_____

64
....

CHAPTER 3

*Instructional
Strategies for
Teaching Learners
with Special Needs*

What will happen next? _____

_____

_____

Number of pages I read during this session: _____

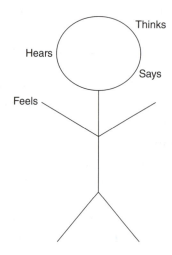

Figure 3.4 Character Map

Audio Recorded Reading 2

Turn on the recording. Listen and point to the words. Pause the recording after reading some pages (paused on page _____).

Three words that looked strange to me: _____

Three words I know: _____

Number of pages I read during this session: _____

Fluency Development Lesson

Purpose

The Fluency Development Lesson (Rasinski, Padak, Linek, & Sturtevant, 1994) is a comprehensive approach to teaching fluency that involves modeling, assisted reading, repeated reading, word study, and home–school involvement. It was recognized by the National Reading Panel (2000) as an effective approach.

Materials

Relatively short reading passages (poems, rhymes, songs, story segments, or other texts) that students read and reread over a brief period of time.

Procedures

65

CHAPTER 3

*Instructional
Strategies for
Teaching Learners
with Special Needs*

1. Introduce a new short text and read it to the students two or three times while they follow along silently.

2. Discuss with the students the nature and content of the passage as well as the quality of your reading of the passage.

3. Read the passage chorally with the students several times. Use antiphonal reading and other variations to create variety and maintain engagement.

4. Organize students into pairs or trios. Each student practices the passage three times while his or her partner listens and provides support and encouragement.

5. Individuals and groups of students perform their reading for the class or other audience, such as another class, a parent visitor, the school principal, or another teacher.

6. With the students, choose four or five interesting words from the text to add to the individual students' word banks and/or the classroom word wall.

7. The students engage in 5–10 minutes of word study activities (e.g., word sorts with word bank words, word walls, definitions of words, word games).

8. The students take a copy of the passage home to practice with parents and other family members.

9. The following day students read the passage from the previous day to you or to a fellow student who checks for accuracy and fluency. Words from the previous day are also read, reread, grouped, and sorted by students and groups of students.

The instructional routine then begins again with step 1, using a new passage.

Vocabulary: Word Predictions

Background

You might select the vocabulary strategy of Word Predictions (Hoyt, 1999) if your instructional goal is concept development or both concept development and comprehension, as word predictions also enhance understanding. In adapting for Tier 2 students, the systematic instruction begins when you introduce the selection, ask what the story might be about, and then demonstrate what "juicy" words might tell about the characters or the meaning of the story. Once they become familiar with the procedure, your students can even do this activity independently or with a partner in order to socially interact as they explore the words.

A Tier 2 student can use the concrete visual scaffold shown below in conversation with you, another adult, or a group of students. Notice that the first column is a place for you or the child to write the "juicy" words the child predicts. Social interaction may be enhanced when you or a peer is the scribe, while the child has an opportunity to talk about the words. After asking why the student chose each word, write the reason briefly. The next column is used to indicate whether the word actually appeared in the text, a process that may be completed either during or after reading. In the next two columns, you or a peer can paraphrase how the student describes the context in which the word appears or why the word may not have appeared. Finally, the last column is a place to add "juicy" words that the child suggests could be added.

Purpose

To focus on vocabulary as a way to activate background knowledge and support reading comprehension.

Materials

A reading selection, either fictional or informational. Students will need some prior knowledge of the topic under study.

Procedures

1. Read the title and ask students, based on the title, what they think the selection may be about.
2. Next, invite them to walk through the text with you, just looking at the pictures.
3. Now, using the pictures and the title of the book as clues, ask students to predict what words they think may be in the selection. Tell them you are interested only in "juicy" words that might tell about the characters or meaning of the story.
4. As students call out words, write them on chart paper. Before writing each word, make sure to ask the student why he or she chose it. You can make this list as long or short as you choose, but 6–10 words are adequate.
5. When your list is complete, either read the story to students or ask them to read it themselves. Tell them to see if the words on the list appear in the text. (If the selection is long, you may want to stop once or twice and visit the list.)
6. After you have read the text, have a brief discussion. Did students enjoy it? What were their favorite parts?

7. Now go back and revisit the words they predicted. Put a check mark next to any words that were used in the text. Discuss where and how these words were used. Ask students to speculate about why the other words might not have appeared in the reading. You might ask if there are any other "juicy" words that should be added to the list.

8. At this point, you have a list of words that can be used for a variety of extension activities that ask students to categorize, act out, retell or write, like List–Group–Label and Word Theater (Newton, Padak, & Rasinski, 2008).

Juicy words	Why did you choose it?	Appear?	If so, in what context?	If not, why?	Juicy words to add

Comprehension: Imagery Strategies

Background

When your instructional goal is to build comprehension skills, adapting your plans from Tier 1 to Tier 2 focuses on easy adaptations that fit with the instructional principles for students with special needs. Comprehension is the process of actively making connections between new information in the text and information that is already known about the topic of the text (Rasinski & Padak, 2008a). Comprehension is about meaning—the meaning of a sentence, a paragraph, or a story. Comprehension, then, is more than simply *decoding* a phrase like "the cat ran up the ladder." It is our own connection to what we know about cats, cats running, the direction of up, what a ladder looks like, and even what would compel a cat to do such a thing. Active meaning-making involves engaging in this type of imagery as well as comparing and contrasting, predicting, and questioning.

Two imagery strategies, Connection to Read-Aloud and Sketch to Stretch, can be adapted for Tier 2 students by focusing on systematic instruction, social interaction, and self-regulation. As you will see, the strategies are extended with adaptations that include demonstrating the images you create in your mind while reading aloud, creating questions for students to follow, and having students talk through their process with peers.

Purpose

To create imagery with a text to enhance textual understanding.

Materials

Paper to pose questions, paper for student sketches, and a book for read-aloud.

Procedures

1. Select a text to read to students aloud.

2. During the read-aloud, talk about an image in your mind that connects with a story. This is the Connection to Read-Aloud. Because you will ask students to sketch what they see, you may also want to draw a quick sketch of your image.

3. Guide students in creating their image by posing questions before, during, or after the read-aloud. Following are some questions you may want to include:
   - Who are the people involved?
   - Where are the characters? What is surrounding them?
   - What movements are the characters making (e.g., sitting, standing, walking)?
   - When does the story take place?
   - What sounds do you hear? What smells do you notice? What feelings are part of the images?

4. Have students sketch their image in order to expand what they see. This is called Sketch to Stretch.

5. Pose questions such as the following for peers to ask in pairs or small groups:
   - What is happening in your sketch?
   - Who is in your sketch?
   - Where does your sketch take place?
   - In what part of the story does your sketch take place?
   - What are some sounds, smells, or feelings in your sketch?
   - How is your sketch similar to or different from my sketch or the illustrations in the story?

   In order to help students self-regulate their creation of images, you can preselect these or other questions and create a concrete visual scaffold by showing the questions on the board or on sheets of paper. If the questions are on paper, students can sketch their images on the other side of the paper. Then students can share their illustrations with each other. As a follow-up, you can invite conversation comparing students' sketches to text illustrations.

With Sketch to Stretch, students have plenty of opportunities to interact socially when they share their illustrations with a small group of peers. Providing questions on a separate sheet of paper helps peers to pose questions and to share insights about a student's illustrations before that student provides his or her own explanation of the sketch.

When students create images in their minds, share these images with their peers, and learn what images their peers create, they can expand their awareness of similarities and differences, another comprehension process essential to understanding. A further adaptation for imagery strategies is to ask children to use graphic organizers for their sketches. For example, character maps or a map with multiple characters can serve as a template. Or a plot map can help students sketch scenes in the story along a continuum. Many more graphic organizers can easily be accessed from the websites listed in Chapter 5.

Adapting Instruction to Meet Students' Needs

We hope that the examples provided in this chapter help you to see how instructional routines can be enhanced through attention to planning for systematic instruction, creating opportunities for social interaction, encouraging self-regulation, and using of visual scaffolds. These adaptations may provide the additional support Tier 2 students need to be successful either in a whole-class setting or in smaller groups. You can use many of these adaptations in classroom learning centers as well. Extra practice in phonemic awareness or phonics/decoding lessons lends itself well to center work. Likewise, students could sort their "juicy" words (vocabulary) or practice reading aloud or listening while reading (fluency). After students have become accustomed to vocabulary and comprehension routines, small groups could complete them independently in a learning center. This extra practice will support student success and enhance Tier 2 students' motivation for reading.

1. This chapter focuses on adapting whole-class reading instruction for Tier 2 students. Given these examples, what other lessons can you incorporate for students with special needs? In what reading element? Together with your colleagues, select one or two instructional strategies you either already use or wish to incorporate into your instruction. Then work through the following questions with your colleagues. Each question aligns with the guiding principles of instruction for students with special needs.

  A. Provide Systematic Instruction

     i. What is the skill that I would like the student to develop at the end of the lesson?

     ii. What is the skill level of this outcome for the majority of students? How do I know?

     iii. What is the skill level of this outcome for Tier 2 students? How do I know?

     iv. What strategies and materials should I adapt and use for Tier 2 students?

     v. How will I monitor the progress of the individuals for whom I adapt the instruction?

  B. Encourage Social Interaction

     i. What prompts can I use to encourage student talk?

     ii. How can I pair up students to work on this strategy?

     iii. How can students work on this strategy in a small group so that each person is involved?

  C. Implement Self-Regulation

     i. What visuals will help students to keep track of what they know and what they are learning next?

     ii. What questions can I ask at the beginning and end of the lesson that will encourage students to think about what they already know?

     iii. What questions can I ask to find out how the strategy is working for each student and what that student might see as a better strategy?

  D. Use Concrete Visual Scaffolds

     i. In what ways can students visualize the content involved with the strategy?

ii. How could students move their bodies to accompany the skill being learned?

iii. What graphic organizers could be helpful?

iv. What images or pictures could enhance the learning outcome?

2. The following chart lists systematic instructional strategies from *Evidence-Based Instruction in Reading: A Professional Development Guide to Phonics Instruction* (Zimmerman, Padak, & Rasinski, 2008). We have either highlighted or added ways to include social interaction, self-regulation, and concrete visual scaffolds when working with these strategies in individual or small-group situations. Finally, we have indicated the strategies that are particularly good fits for Tier 2 students. Overall, the chart shows what these concepts mean in the context of phonics instruction for students with special needs. (*Note:* You and your colleagues may want to create a similar chart for the other elements of reading instruction.)

Book Club

Phonics Strategies with Suggestions for Systematic Instruction, Social Interaction, Self-Regulation, and Concrete Visual Scaffolds

Phonics Strategy	Systematic Instruction	Social Interaction	Self-Regulation	Concrete Visual Scaffolds
Action Phonics	Plan for children to learn letter–sound relationships by presenting a sequence of cards with letters on one side and action words on the other.	Children say the action words. They can also be encouraged to tell each other the words. Then they perform the actions together. Alternatively, several action words can be listed on the board, each child can select one, and the rest of the class can guess which action the child is portraying.	Children restate how action phonics will help them decode unknown words.	Children move their bodies in order to build memories of letters and sounds. Action phonics cards serve as visual reminders.
Target Letter Transport	Plan for children to locate letter–sound relationships at the beginning, middle, and end of words through a sequence beginning with first hearing the initial sound and then identifying the letter.	Children say the letter sounds together and with the teacher.	Children identify difficult words by whether the difficulty is in the beginning, middle, or end. They can also identify whether the letters they see are consonants, vowels, or blends.	Children hold up their letter cards when there is a word that begins or ends with the letter of interest.
Onsets and Rimes	Plan to introduce concepts of *onset* and *rime*. Then demonstrate how to use them to construct words.	Children construct words and discover new identifiable "chunks" in words as teams.	Children identify whether common rimes are easy or difficult for them to find in new words.	Children use a Venn diagram to compare ending consonants of the same short vowel rimes, different short vowel rimes, or rimes with the same written vowel symbol.
Three-Day and Five-Day Rime Time Routines	Plan to introduce rimes and create a routine for learning about them.	Children chorally read poems; teams identify certain letters, blends, and digraphs; poetry partners perform poems.	Children use a chart to keep track of child-identified rimes and known rimes.	Children use objects or pictures that correspond with poems.

Phonics Strategy	Systematic Instruction	Social Interaction	Self-Regulation	Concrete Visual Scaffolds
Using Rimes to Decode by Analogy	Plan to draw students' attention to a rime in a new word, connect it to a known word, and show students how to make letter substitutions.	Children work together to substitute letters in known words to make new words.	Children keep known and new words on a personal list.	Children use magnetic letters, view word wall words, and organize their own words into new and known.
Whiteboard Word Families	Plan to introduce rimes and create a routine for introducing and demonstrating rimes.	Children locate words in a poem or story that contain the same rime.	Children keep known and new words on a personal list.	Children draw circles around word families.

Take a look at this chart with your colleagues, and answer the following questions:

A. Which self-monitoring or concrete visual scaffolding ideas could I use right away with a student I have in mind?

_____

_____

_____

_____

B. How can I innovate with my students with special needs, given some of the ideas in the chart?

_____

_____

_____

_____

CHAPTER 4

Beyond Strategies

*I*n earlier chapters, we explored how children with special needs learn to become skilled readers and some of the best instructional strategies and assessments to support that practice. The strategies we described are adapted for targeted instruction in Tier II, and the assessments inform how Tier II students respond to the interventions. In this chapter, we consider issues that go "beyond strategies." In particular, we provide some basic information about English language learners (ELLs) under the "special needs" umbrella. (A separate volume in the *Evidence-Based Instruction in Reading* series [Wisniewski, Fawcett, Padak, & Rasinski, in press] addresses instruction for ELLs in more depth.) We also offer suggestions for helping parents to conduct at-home reading activities and to understand special education guidelines.

English Language Learners as Students with Special Needs

Did you ever study a foreign language in school? If so, you may recall feeling inadequate, excited, and confused as you explored a whole new way of talking and thinking. This is how many children from other cultures feel as they enter American classrooms. Your instruction may be the first time a student reads from left to right if reading in his or her native language is right to left. Or you may instruct the child in consonant blends like *th* that do not occur in his or her native language. Or perhaps the stories this student reads in your classroom contain unfamiliar cultural references.

Students whose native language is not English may struggle when learning to read in English. Perhaps their *ability* to learn appears comparable to that of their peers, but they lag in gaining English reading *skills* when compared to their native-English-speaking peers. It is important to differentiate ability from skill in order to attend to student progress in reading. Ability includes cognitive domains such as processing speed, working memory, and problem solving. Reading skills include knowledge of letter–sound correspondences, vocabulary knowledge, and comprehension. If an ELL appears to have average processing speed and can identify letter–sound correspondences in English but cannot retell a simple story, then the student may need more targeted instruction in reading comprehension.

Therefore, under the umbrella of students with special needs, ELLs need more targeted instruction that allows for the reading gap between them and their peers to lessen. Given the cultural and linguistic diversity of our population, your classroom may have children from several countries. How do you plan instruction that reaches each individual learner?

Children raised in bilingual homes have unique advantages as well as unique challenges. These children bring rich background experiences that can be tapped to enhance everyone's learning. They know how to move between two languages, integrating sounds and meanings into new words and grammatical structures. Their natural manipulation of two languages promotes higher-level thinking. Yet ELLs sometimes feel lost in the unfamiliar linguistic and academic world in which they find themselves. Fitzgerald and Graves (2004) describe this feeling:

> Many English-language learners bring an array of emotions to our classrooms that often are not evident on the surface. The student who is afraid that his talk will sound funny to others may hide his self-consciousness. The student who does not fully understand what is said may hold a steady gaze and outwardly appear confident or even cocky. (p. 3)

Fortunately, everything we have learned so far about how to teach reading to students with special needs applies to both first- and second-language learners: ELLs need systematic instruction, social interaction, self-regulation skills, and concrete visual scaffolds. Following are four ideas to keep in mind as you plan instruction for second-language learners:

1. Provide *systematic instruction* in the essential components of reading. A planned sequence of instruction aids in determining the reading outcome, student background knowledge, strategies to implement, how well the instruction is going, and what to revise. For example, if the outcome is to learn words, then a volunteer or tutor needs to determine what English words the ELL knows before determining what visual–verbal associations to make for vocabulary learning.

2. Provide *social interaction* while making progress in reading. This can come in the form of peer interaction, where peers have opportunities to talk through reading, or in individual instruction, where the student has opportunities to talk through the process. Either way, ELLs need to be introduced to a wide range of vocabulary and have frequent opportunities to converse as well as to hear English texts read orally in order to

build vocabulary and deepen comprehension. Sheltered instruction in English (described following this list) also uses group work as an important element for helping ELLs become members of the classroom society; it also provides both receptive and expressive language learning opportunities that ELLs need in order to build their understanding of the English language.

3. Build *skills in self-regulating* reading progress. Self-regulation is metacognitive; students think through their thinking. More specifically, students can identify their strengths as learners, the task (e.g., reading a story), strategies to accomplish the task (e.g., look at the cover, predict what might happen, and then clarify their prediction during the reading), and how the strategies worked (e.g., predictions were accurate, but unknown words caused problems). ELLs then become responsible for their learning and become active learners of English.

4. Provide *concrete visual scaffolds* associated with their reading strategies. Like other students with special needs, ELLs benefit from a strategy they can see while learning, whether it is in the form of pictures, objects, or graphic organizers. These nonverbal cues can also include graphs, pictures, maps, displays, action to dramatize meaning, and other concrete materials.

These ideas are further addressed in sheltered instruction for ELLs (e.g., Echevarria, Vogt, & Short, 2004). Sheltered instruction is an approach to teaching ELLs that provides access to grade-level content, while also promoting the development of English language proficiency. For example, in using *If You Give a Mouse a Cookie* (Numeroff, 1985) for reading comprehension, first assess and build on students' interests and prior knowledge, including cultural knowledge (e.g., What are other words for *cookie*? What kinds of cookies do you like?). Second, plan for concrete visual scaffolds, which can include items or pictures of items from the story (such as cookie, milk, and broom). Third, plan for social interaction before, during, or after the story. This could include each student having an item from the story and forming a circle with the items to predict the story's sequence of events or to depict how this type of story returns to the starting point. Finally, plan how ELLs could self-monitor by adding a circle graphic organizer that students could complete or a checklist for hearing each item in the story as the item is read aloud.

Reading Activities at Home

Both practitioners and researchers have long recognized the importance of parental involvement in children's early reading achievement. Children whose families encourage at-home literacy activities have greater phonemic awareness and decoding skills (Burgess, 1999), greater reading achievement in the elementary grades (Cooter, Marrin, & Mills-House, 1999), and advanced oral language development (Senechal, LeFevre, & Thomas, 1998). Family literacy professionals often point out that parents are their children's first and most important teachers. Instructing parents to simply "Read to your child" may be a start, but it is not enough. Parents need specific suggestions and guidelines about what to do and how to respond to their child's literacy development. In this section, we offer guidelines and some sample activities for home involvement programs and practices that foster children's reading development. For more information on parental involvement, see the parent/family involvement book in this series.

Most parents do not share teachers' knowledge of reading, the reading process, and how to teach students with special needs. Parents may also feel frustrated with helping their child to read at home. Therefore, it is essential that teachers understand parents' realities, while also helping them to understand the basic principles of Response to Intervention (RTI), which are being proactive, matching student abilities and needs with instruction, solving problems, and practicing reading daily. Some questions to ask parents may include these:

- What reading does your child do at home?
- When do you hear your child read aloud?
- What is your child interested in reading?
- What are your daily routines? How does or could reading fit into them?
- What ideas do you have for helping your child become a better reader at home?

These questions will provide you with a basis for communication in order to offer support for reading activities at home.

Teachers know that home involvement can provide rich opportunities for children to develop as readers. Moreover, it's important for children to see reading and literacy activities as worthwhile and critical outside of school as well as within school walls. Yet home involvement programs are sometimes frustrating for teachers, parents, and children alike. Our work with supporting home involvement programs has led us to several design characteristics that must be present for such a program to be successful (Rasinski, Padak, & Fawcett, 2010):

- *Use proven and effective strategies:* Many parents have limited time to devote to working with their children, so at-home activities must be focused on ideas that have been proven to make a positive difference in children's reading achievement. At-home reading sessions should be relatively brief, probably no more than 15–20 minutes, perhaps less for younger children.

- *Use authentic reading texts:* Reading aloud to children allows parents to model fluent reading as well as providing opportunities to discuss books and even point out text features. Similarly, when parents read with their children or listen to their children read, children grow as readers. These simple activities—read to, read with, and listen to children—are powerful ways to promote reading achievement. What about texts? We believe it's essential for them to be authentic. For young readers, texts such as simple poems, song lyrics, jokes, or jump rope rhymes work very well. Older students might help parents to select books and articles of interest.

- *Provide materials:* We believe that some parent involvement plans fail because parents lack appropriate texts or the time or resources to acquire them. The easiest solution is to provide parents and children with reading materials. In addition to looking for materials in books, teachers will find the Internet to be a treasure trove of wonderful materials for students and their parents to read. (See "Parent Activities" in Chapter 5 for examples.)

With these principles in mind, you can develop some simple home reading activities for phonemic awareness, phonics, fluency, vocabulary, and comprehension.

Practice Phonemic Awareness

Talk to parents about rehearsing sounds of spoken language with their child to show how they blend together to create words. The best way for children to learn about how the sound system of language works is to play with the sounds. Here are some phonemic awareness activities that you can use during classroom instruction and also suggest to parents (Day, Dommer, Mraz, & Padak, 2002). These activities help students with special needs at home.

- Sing little songs with the child; recite nursery rhymes together. This works particularly well if the stories or rhymes are short. Stress the rhymes and alliterations found in the poem, for example:

  Hickory Dickory **DOCK**

  The mouse ran up the **CLOCK**

- Look for books in the library or in bookstores that have rhyming words. A children's librarian can help you to locate good books. Read these with the child. Emphasize the rhyming words.

- Use a picture dictionary. Look at the pages with the child. Ask the child to point to objects on the page that begin with sounds you say. For example, you could ask, "Can you find something on the page that starts with /d/?" Or you could point to something on the page and ask the child, "What sound does this begin with?" or "Does this begin with /d/?"

- Play Sound Scavenger Hunt. (In the classroom, this works well during transition times, for example, as a way of dismissing students from a large group one by one. Outside the classroom, this works well in the car.) For example, say, "Let's find something that begins with the sound /s/." Or "I see a pencil. What sound does *pencil* begin with?" When the child can find beginning sounds easily, the same game can be played with ending sounds.

- Play rhyming word games. Ask the child to listen to pairs of words. If the word pair rhymes, ask the child to clap or to sit down or to jump up. For example, say, "cat, fat," "cat, dog," or "dog, fog."

- Play the game I Say. Use this frame to play with words. You say one simple word. The child says another word that rhymes:

  "I say **bat.** You say _____."

  "I say **tree.** You say _____."

- Collect pictures from magazines, newspapers, or junk mail. Ask the child to find things in the pictures that begin with certain sounds. For example, you might ask the child to find things that begin with /p/. The child could make a sound book by cutting these pictures out and pasting them in a homemade book (scrapbook). The book may become part of the child's home library.

- Using the same magazines, newspapers, and junk mail, you cut out some pictures. Give the child three of them, two that begin with the same sound and one that does not. Ask the child to find the one picture that does not belong.
- Play the game Change the Word. Give the child a simple word. Ask the child to change the beginning sound of the word to make a new word. For example, you could say, "My word is *boat*. Change /b/ to /k/. What is your word?"

Develop Phonics Skills

Applying decoding skills is a problem-solving process. Talk to parents about the importance of allowing the child time to think when he or she pauses at an unknown word rather than automatically supplying the word whenever the child is "stuck." It is also beneficial to provide parents with several prompts that they can use to encourage the child to engage in the problem solving. Parents have a tendency to over-rely on the age-old prompt "Sound it out," so it is helpful for teachers to provide them with some more effective alternatives:

- "Get your mouth ready for the beginning sound."
- "What letter do you see at the beginning [or end] of the word? What sound does it stand for?"
- Ask the child to pronounce the first sound in a word and then say, "Now that you have the first sound, say more of that word."
- "Can you think of a word that would make sense here and begins with these letters?"

Practice Fluent Reading

Talk to parents about the importance of fluency routines. Explain that, although students may recognize words that they are reading, their oral reading may be slow and choppy. Fluency routines will enhance the identification of words, while also constructing meaning of larger, multiple-word units of texts. Encourage parents to do some simple activities such as the following while reading books, newspapers, or magazines with their children:

- Ask the child what books he or she enjoys. Have the child repeat reading those books aloud to interested peers, family, neighbors, and friends.

- Have the child select a book for paired reading with a parent or another good reader. Tell the parent to either slightly lead or slightly follow while reading aloud, based on the child's skill.
- Have the child share reading by reading one page and then having an adult or another good reader read the next page.
- Find out what tools are available at home to record a child reading. This may be an audiotape recorder, a videotape recorder, or a free software program on a computer (e.g., http://audacity.sourceoforge.net). Have the child record the reading of a book of interest, and then play it back while the child reads the story again along with the recording.

It will also be important to show parents how to do paired reading and shared reading with their children. Fast Start, a more comprehensive home involvement routine we developed and have been studying for several years (Padak & Rasinski, 2004a, 2004b, 2005; Stevenson, Rasinski, & Padak, 2006), is also a highly effective way to support children's fluency development and overall reading achievement at home. The Fast Start routine has four basic steps:

- Parent (or more able reader: sibling, grandparent, babysitter, etc.) and child sit together. Parent reads a short text to the child several times, pointing to words as they are read.
- Parent and child read the text together and aloud. They also do this several times.
- Child reads the text independently. Parent listens, provides support if necessary, and praises child's reading.
- Parent and child do a brief, developmentally appropriate literacy-related activity based on the text.

Texts for the Fast Start routine are short poems, jump rope rhymes, and songs. Many resources for locating these are listed in Chapter 5 of the fluency text in this series (Padak & Rasinski, 2008). Activities are simple to develop. We recommend that you develop three sets of activities that can be used with any text. One set can focus on concepts about print, a second set can address phonemic awareness issues, and the third set can relate to beginning reading. Then you can simply tell each family which set of activities will benefit the child most.

Explore Vocabulary

Talk to parents about the importance of embedding *word awareness* in their children's literacy experiences. Explain that word awareness is really curiosity about words, where they come from, what they mean, and how they can be used. Make sure parents understand that you are not referring to rote memorization of a specific list of "important" words. Instead, you want their children to establish a habit of mind about words. Encourage parents to do some simple home activities that can help with vocabulary development:

- Place words on their objects in the home. For example, label objects such as a cabinet, refrigerator, and stove. This may be especially beneficial for those learning words in English as their second language.

- Use word magnets on the refrigerator. When sharing time with a child in the kitchen, the parent can ask what words the child knows, kind of knows, or does not know and then move the magnets to different spaces on the refrigerator door. Discussions about the words can lead to learning word meanings and creating sentences.

- Wonder out loud about the meaning of new words that the parent comes across when reading the newspaper, watching television, or reading mail. Then take a moment to look up the word in a dictionary or on the Internet.

- Pause now and then during shared reading to talk about the story. When finished, ask the child to describe a favorite part or favorite character. Then tell the child to find an interesting word; you find one, too. Talk about these words.

- Make trips to the local library a routine. We learn most new vocabulary through reading, and we read more widely when we choose books of high interest to us. Allow enough time for children to browse through and choose from the hundreds of appealing children's books available on the shelves.

Improve Text Comprehension

Talk with parents about good text comprehension. Explain that it is a process of actively connecting what the reader already knows about the topic of the text with the actual text. To encourage active connections, parents can ask questions like these:

- What does this story make you think of?
- Does this story remind you of another story we read?
- Does anyone you know remind you of this character?

Other questions parents can ask may involve predicting, clarifying, identifying events, and sequencing events:

- Ask your child to read the title of the book and look at the image on the front of the book. Then ask, "What do you think this story is about?" After reading a few pages, clarify the prediction and then predict again: "Is this what you thought would happen? What might happen next?"
- Ask the child one or more of the "5 W's" while reading: "Who is in the story?" "What is happening?" "When does it take place?" "Where are the characters?" "What problems are the characters dealing with?" "How are they solving these problems?"
- Draw a timeline of the story with your child, identifying three or more events. Ask, "What happened first? Next? Next? How did it end?"

Special Needs and Special Education

In Chapter 1, we explored the difference between students with special needs that can be met in the general education classroom and those best served through special education services. We presented the RTI framework, where about 10–15% of the students in a class need adapted instruction and careful progress monitoring to determine their "response" to the "intervention." Development in reading skills is the ultimate goal of RTI for students with special needs.

However, approximately 5% of students will not progress in reading with targeted, evidence-based instruction in the regular classroom. These students need intensive, individual instruction in reading outside the classroom under the umbrella of either general education or special education. These are often students with learning disabilities. But what classifies them as students with learning disabilities?

A learning disability can be diagnosed one of three ways. As we discussed in Chapter 1, the first way to diagnose a learning disability is the traditional way: through analyzing the difference between a student's abilities as measured on a test of intelligence and his or her reading skills as measured on a test of achievement. This method has been termed the *discrepancy model* of learning disability diagnosis.

The Individuals with Disabilities Education Act (IDEA) of 2004 introduced a second way to diagnose a learning disability that is based on a student's response to classroom intervention. In this instance, a team of professionals uses the progress-monitoring information collected as part of Tier 2 instruction. One or more members of the team may also observe the child during instruction. These data are used to determine, first, that the student is not responding to targeted, evidence-based interventions and, second, that the child has a learning disability. The third way of diagnosing a learning disability combines both the discrepancy model and RTI (Scruggs & Mastropieri, 2002).

Parents may ask you questions about whether their child has a learning disability and what process is used to identify learning disability in your school. First, explain the RTI model. If their child has special needs in reading and is therefore in Tier 2 of the model, explain that the process includes these steps:

1. Identify students who need targeted assistance in the classroom.
2. Plan the assistance based on the learning outcomes for the child's grade level and the child's need in reading (e.g., in phonemic awareness, phonics, fluency, vocabulary, and/or comprehension).
3. Keep the same reading goals as in Tier 1 instruction and modify the instructional approach. For example, if children in your classroom are engaging in audio-recorded reading to build reading skills, explain that students in Tier 2 will use a character map or plot map while following along with the story.
4. Monitor the progress in the reading element.
5. Adapt instruction based on the progress monitoring.

Next, describe what will happen if the child is not making progress based on the research-based targeted instruction that you implement. Further assessment may reveal that the child needs to have more individualized instruction and/or to be tested for a learning disability. After you find out from your school psychologist or principal which of the three ways is used in your school for diagnosing a learning disability, then let the parent know.

When talking with parents about their child, remember that they could be experiencing frustration at home with helping their child read. Before explaining the RTI model or the processes you use for targeting instruction, find out what the parents know about the process and what expectations they may have. Be sure to make notes for yourself and let the parents know when you will follow up with them so that they get timely feedback on their questions and concerns regarding their child's reading progress.

Book Club   Professional Development Suggestions

ACED: Analysis, Clarification, Extension, Discussion

I. REFLECTION (10–15 minutes)

ANALYSIS

- What, for you, were the most interesting and/or important ideas in this chapter regarding students with special needs?

- What information was new to you?

CLARIFICATION

- Did anything surprise you? Confuse you?

EXTENSION

- What questions do you have?

II. DISCUSSION (30 minutes)

- Form groups of 4–6 members.
- Appoint a *facilitator (timer)* and *recorder*.
- Share responses. Make sure that each person has shared his or her responses to each category (Analysis/Clarification/Extension).
- Help each other with any areas of confusion.
- Answer and/or discuss questions raised by group members.
- On chart paper, the recorder should summarize the main discussion points and identify issues or questions the group would like to raise for general discussion.

III. APPLICATION (10 minutes)

- Based on your reflection and discussion, how might you apply what you have learned from this chapter regarding students with special needs?

_____

_____

_____

_____

English Language Learners

Book Club

Think of the ELLs you currently teach. Discuss the ideas in this chapter and keep in mind the corresponding questions while planning instruction for ELLs. Plan to share your ideas in your professional development group.

a. In planning systematic instruction:
    i. How can you determine what they already know about letter–sound relationships?
    ii. How can you determine what vocabulary they already know?
    iii. How can you determine their cultural knowledge in order to assist you in explaining reading activities?

b. In improving social interaction experiences:

    i. How can you determine what gestures they know in English?

    ii. How can you provide them with opportunities to talk in English with their peers?

    iii. How can you assist them in becoming members of the classroom society?

c. In building skills in self-regulation:

    i. How can you help them to determine their reading strengths?

    ii. How can you help them to understand the reading tasks?

    iii. How can you help them to select strategies for the task and self-assess their progress?

d. In providing concrete visual scaffolds:

    i. How can you determine what graphic organizers will assist in their reading?

    ii. How can you determine what objects to use in reading activities?

    iii. How can you determine what other graphs, pictures, displays, or actions to use to dramatize meaning in reading activities?

Book Club

Students with Special Needs

Think of the students with special needs that you currently teach. Select one of more of those students who need targeted instruction in one of the reading elements. Then complete one or both of the following charts with your insights and plans for targeted instruction.

Curriculum Alignment

Check one or more reading element:

1. **Phonemic Awareness**
2. **Phonics**
3. **Fluency**
4. **Vocabulary**
5. **Comprehension**

Component	What is...	What should be...
Curriculum		
Instruction		
Materials		
Assessment		
Home Connection		

Source: Adapted from *Literacy Leadership for Grades 5–12, by E. Taylor and V. Collins, 2003.* Alexandria, VA: Association for Supervision and Curriculum Development.

Goal Planning

Goal _____

Plans by _____ Date _____

Action Steps	Materials/Resources	Evaluation

CHAPTER 5

Resources

*I*n this final chapter, we offer resources for classroom activities and for your own further learning. Both web-based and print resources are provided.

Websites (all active as of August 2010)

Concrete Visual Strategies

Balajthy, E. (2005). Text-to-speech software for helping struggling readers. *http://www.readingonline.org/articles/art_index.asp?HREF=balajthy2/index.html*

Kibby, M. W., & Scott, L. (2002). Using computer simulations to teach decision making in reading diagnostic assessment for remediation. *http://www.readingonline.org/articles/art_index.asp?HREF=kibby/index.html*

Oakley, G. (2003). Improving oral reading fluency (and comprehension) through the creation of talking books. *http://www.readingonline.org/articles/art_index.asp?HREF=oakley/index.html*

Graphic Organizers

Graphic organizers from Region 15. *http://www.region15.org/page.php?pid=107*

Graphic organizers from Scholastic. *http://teacher.scholastic.com/lessonplans/graphicorg/index.htm*

Graphic organizers from Teacher Vision. *http://www.teachervision.fen.com/graphic-organizers/printable/6293.html*

Graphic organizers from Teach-nology. *http://www.teach-nology.com/worksheets/graphic*

Software

Audio-recorded reading is a fluency strategy that provides individual and independent practice in reading. Audio-recorded reading can be implemented in three ways: A student can read with a pre-manufactured audio recording of the book, with an audio recording created by a peer or adult, or with an audio recording created by the student. Recordings can be made using an audiotape recorder or a computer (podcasts). Some computers come with software that records audio through a built-in or external microphone. Others have a microphone but do not have software for recording. *Audacity*, which is free software for recording and editing sounds, can be downloaded from *http://audacity.sourceforge.net*.

Websites for Phonics Fun

Between the Lions from PBS Kids. Play games with words and learn spelling from fun characters at the same time.
http://pbskids.org/games

Gamequarium/Free Phonics Games. This site allows you to customize games, like Hangman, for your students.
http://www.gamequarium.com/phonics28.html

Phonics Games—Free to Print and Play. This collection of free phonics and word games is available for downloading and printing.
http://www.adrianbruce.com/reading/games.htm

BBC Schools—Words and Pictures. Colorful games, printable pages, animations, and other activities help 5- to 7-year-olds with reading and phonics.
http://www.bbc.co.uk/schools/wordsandpictures

Softschools—Free Phonics Worksheets and Games. These free phonics games, flashcards, and online activities for kids include short vowel sounds and long vowel sounds for preschool and kindergarten.
http://www.softschools.com/language_arts/phonics

Clifford Interactive Storybooks. These interactive storybooks feature Clifford The Big Red Dog plus phonics fun, games, and stories for early readers.
http://www.teacher.scholastic.com/clifford1

Literacy Center Phonics. This site teaches letter formations and letter sounds in English, Spanish, French, and German.
http://www.literacycenter.net

Phonics Game Show. With a *Jeopardy*-like game board, students are quizzed about certain phonics rules and other aspects of decoding and the alphabetic principle.
http://www.surfnetkids.com/quiz/phonics

Special Education, Response to Intervention, and the Reading Teacher's Role

Dumont-Willis guide to the identification of learning disabilities. Sample information is available free of charge at this site.
http://alpha.fdu.edu/psychology/guide_to_identification_of.htm

International Dyslexia Association. This site provides a wealth of information, materials, and other resources for working with students having significant difficulties in learning to read.
http://www.interdys.org
   See in particular:

- Interventions. *http://www.interdys.org/InsInt.htm*
- Frequently asked questions. *http://www.interdys.org/FAQ.htm#*
- Research. *http://www.interdys.org/ResearchArticles.htm*

International Reading Association (IRA).
http://www.reading.org
   See in particular:

- Complete list of IRA resources related to RTI. *http://www.reading.org/ Resources/ResourcesByTopic/ResponseToIntervention/Overview.aspx*
- New roles in Response to Intervention: Creating success for schools and children: A collection of fact sheets. *http://www.reading.org/ downloads/resources/rti_role_definitions.pdf*
- Reading teachers play key role in successful RTI approaches. *http:// www.reading.org/downloads/resources/IDEA_RTI_teachers_role.pdf*
- Position statement: The role of reading instruction in addressing the overrepresentation of minority children in special education in the United States. *http://www.reading.org/General/AboutIRA/Position Statements/MinoritiesSpecialEdPosition.aspx*

Intervention Central is a website that provides teachers and school psychologists with information and resources for assessing and teaching students with significant reading difficulties.
http://www.interventioncentral.org

LD Online, from WETA Public Television in Virginia, calls itself "the leading website on learning disabilities, learning disorders and differences."
http://www.ldonline.org

Mellard, D. (2002). *Understanding Responsiveness to Intervention in learning disabilities determination.* National Research Center on Learning Disabilities.
http://www.nrcld.org/about/publications/papers/mellard.pdf

Response to Intervention law and perspectives for teachers and parents from Wright's Law.
http://www.wrightslaw.com/info/rti.index.htm

Response to Intervention resources from the National Center on Response to Intervention.
http://www.rti4success.org

School Psychology Resources Online, a website maintained by Sandra Steingart, provides resources for psychologists, educators, and parents.
http://www.schoolpsychology.net

Parent Activities

Reading activities for parents and their children from Reading Is Fundamental.
http://www.rif.org/parents/activities/default.mspx

Reading activities for parents and their children from Reading Rockets.
http://www.readingrockets.org/article/c71

Reading tips for parents from Family Education.
http://school.familyeducation.com/reading-tips/parents-and-school/33582.html

Print Teacher Resources

RTI and Students with Special Needs in Reading

Allington, R. L. (2005). *What really matters for struggling readers: Designing research-based programs.* (2nd ed.). New York: Allyn & Bacon.

Allington, R. (2008). *What really matters in RTI: Research-based designs.* Boston: Allyn & Bacon.

Applegate, M., Applegate, A. J., & Modla, V. B. (2009). "She's my best reader; she just can't comprehend": Studying the relationship between fluency and comprehension. *The Reading Teacher, 62,* 512–521.

Batsche, G., Elliott, J., Graden, J., Grimes, J., Kovaleski, J., Prasse, D., ... & Tilly, W., III. (2005). *Response to Intervention: Policy considerations and implementation.* Alexandria, VA: National Association of State Directors of Special Education.

Bauer, E. (2009). Informed additive literacy instruction for ELLs. *The Reading Teacher, 62,* 446–448.

Bauer, E., & Manyak, P. C. (2008). Creating language-rich instruction for English-Language Learners. *The Reading Teacher, 62,* 176–178.

Fuchs, D., & Fuchs, L. (2006). Introduction to Response to Intervention: What, why, and how valid is it? *Reading Research Quarterly, 41,* 93–99.

Gersten, R., & Dimino, J. (2006). RTI (Response to Intervention): Rethinking special education for students with reading difficulties (yet again). *Reading Research Quarterly, 41,* 99–108.

Klingner, J., & Edwards, P. (2006). Cultural considerations with Response to Intervention models. *Reading Research Quarterly, 41,* 108–117.

Lyons, C. A. (1989). Reading Recovery: An effective early intervention program that can prevent mislabeling children as learning disabled. *ERS Spectrum, 7*(4), 3–9.

Lyons, C. A. (1991). Helping a learning-disabled child enter the literate world. In D. DeFord, C. A. Lyons, & G. S. Pinnell (Eds.), *Bridges to literacy: Learning from Reading Recovery.* Exeter, NH: Heinemann.

Lyons, C. A. (1994). Reading Recovery and learning disability: Issues, challenges, and implications. *Literacy, Teaching and Learning, 1*(1), 109–120.

Lyons, C. (2003). *Teaching struggling readers.* Portsmouth, NH: Heinemann.

Mesmer, E. M., & Mesmer, H. E. (2008). Response to Intervention (RTI): What teachers of reading need to know. *The Reading Teacher, 62,* 280–290.

Rasinski, T. V., Padak, N., & Fawcett, G. (2010). *Teaching children who find reading difficult* (4th ed.). Boston: Allyn & Bacon.

Shanahan, T. (2008). Implications of RTI for the reading teacher. In D. Fuchs, L. S. Fuchs, & S. Vaughn (Eds.), *Response to Intervention* (pp. 105–122). Newark, DE: International Reading Association.

Strickland, D., Ganske, K., & Monroe, J. (2002). *Supporting struggling readers and writers.* Portland, ME: Stenhouse.

Effective Instruction in Reading

Beck, I. L., & McKeown, M. G. (2006). *Improving comprehension with Questioning the Author.* New York: Scholastic.

Block, C. C., Gambrell, L., & Pressley, M. (Eds.). (2002). *Improving reading comprehension: Rethinking research, theory, and classroom practice.* San Francisco: Jossey-Bass.

Block, C. C., & Pressley, M. (Eds.). (2001). *Comprehension instruction: Research-based best practices.* New York: Guilford.

Daniels, H. (1994). *Literature circles: Voice and choice in the student-centered classroom.* Portland, ME: Stenhouse.

Day, J. P., Spiegel, D. L., McLellan, J., & Brown, V. B. (2002). *Moving forward with literature circles.* New York: Scholastic.

Harvey, S. (1998). *Nonfiction matters: Reading, writing, and research in grades 3–8.* Portland, ME: Stenhouse.

Harvey, S., & Goudvis, A. (2000). *Strategies that work.* Portland, ME: Stenhouse.

Hoyt, L. (1998). *Revisit, reflect, retell: Strategies for improving reading comprehension.* Portsmouth, NH: Heinemann.

Invernizzi, M., Juel, C., & Rosemary, C. (1996). A community volunteer tutorial that works. *The Reading Teacher, 50,* 304–311.

Koskinen, P. S., Blum, I. H., Bisson, S. A., Phillips, S. M., Creamer, T. S., & Baker, T. K. (1999). Shared reading, books, and audiotapes: Supporting diverse students in school and at home. *The Reading Teacher, 52,* 430–444.

Kuhn, M. (2004). Helping students become accurate, expressive readers: Fluency instruction for small groups. *The Reading Teacher, 58,* 333–344.

Kuhn, M. R., & Stahl, S. A. (2000). *Fluency: A review of developmental and remedial practices* (CIERA Report 2-008). Ann Arbor, MI: Center for the Improvement of Early Reading Achievement. Available online at http://www.ciera.org/library/reports/inquiry-2/2-008/2-008.html

Martinez, M., & Roser, N. (1985). Read it again: The value of repeated readings during story time. *The Reading Teacher, 38,* 782–786.

Martinez, M., Roser, N., & Strecker, S. (1999). "I never thought I could be a star": A readers theatre ticket to reading fluency. *The Reading Teacher, 52,* 326–334.

McLaughlin, M. (2003). *Guided comprehension in the primary grades.* Newark, DE: International Reading Association.

McLaughlin, M., & Allen, M. B. (2002). *Guided comprehension in action: A teaching model for grades 3–8.* Newark, DE: International Reading Association.

McLaughlin, M., & DeVoogd, G. (2004). *Critical literacy: Enhancing students' comprehension of text.* New York: Scholastic.

Miller, D. (2002). *Reading with meaning: Teaching comprehension in the primary grades.* Portland, ME: Stenhouse.

Opitz, M. F., & Rasinski, T. V. (1998). *Good-bye Round Robin: 25 effective oral reading strategies.* Portsmouth, NH: Heinemann.

Padak, N., & Rasinski, T. (2008). The games children play. *The Reading Teacher, 62,* 363–365.

Perfect, K. A. (1999). Rhyme and reason: Poetry for the heart and head. *The Reading Teacher, 52,* 728–737.

Prescott, J. O. (2003). The power of reader's theater. *Instructor, 112*(5), 22–27.

Rasinski, T. V. (2003). *The fluent reader: Oral reading strategies for building word recognition, fluency, and comprehension.* New York: Scholastic.

Rasinski, T. V., & Hoffman, T. V. (2003). Theory and research into practice: Oral reading in the school literacy curriculum. *Reading Research Quarterly, 38,* 510–522.

Rasinski, T. V., & Padak, N. (2008). *From phonics to fluency: Effective teaching of decoding and reading fluency in the elementary school* (2nd ed.). New York: Longman.

Rasinski, T. V., Padak, N. D., Church, B. W., Fawcett, G., Hendershot, J., Henry, J., ... & Roskos, K. A. (Eds.). (2000). *Teaching comprehension and exploring multiple literacies: Strategies from* The Reading Teacher. Newark, DE: International Reading Association.

Rasinski, T. V., Padak, N., & Fawcett, G. (2010). *Teaching children who find reading difficult* (4th ed.). New York: Prentice Hall.

Rasinski, T., Rupley, W. H., & Nichols, W. (2008). Two essential ingredients: Phonics and fluency getting to know each other. *The Reading Teacher, 62,* 257–260.

Shaywitz, S. (2005). *Overcoming dyslexia: A new and complete science-based program for reading problems at any level.* New York: Vintage.

Stone, C. A., Silliman, E. R., Ehren, B. J., & Apel, K. (Eds.). (2004). *Handbook of language and literacy: Development and disorders.* New York: Guilford.

Wilfong, L. G. (2008). Building fluency, word-recognition ability, and confidence in struggling readers: The Poetry Academy. *The Reading Teacher, 62,* 4–13.

Wilhelm, J. D. (1996). *You gotta BE the book: Teaching engaged and reflective reading with adolescents.* New York: Teachers College Press.

Wilhelm, J. D. (2001). *Improving comprehension with think-aloud strategies.* New York: Scholastic.

Wilhelm, J. D. (2002). *Action strategies for deepening comprehension: Role plays, text structure, tableaux, talking statues, and other enrichment techniques that engage students with text.* New York: Scholastic.

Wilhelm, J., Baker, T., & Dube, J. (2001). *Strategic reading: Guiding students to lifelong literacy.* Portsmouth, NH: Heinemann.

Worthy, J., & Broaddus, K. (2002). Fluency beyond the primary grades: From group performance to silent, independent reading. *The Reading Teacher, 55,* 334–343.

Worthy, J., & Prater, K. (2002). "I thought about it all night": Readers Theater for reading fluency and motivation. *The Reading Teacher, 56,* 294–297.

Book Club Ideas

*T*hroughout the book, you have seen icons indicating activities or discussion points that lend themselves to book club conversations. We hope you and your colleagues will take advantage of these opportunities. Our experience has taught us that learning from and with each other is a powerful way to promote innovation. In this appendix, we provide additional questions and ideas for discussion. They are organized according to the chapters in the book.

Introduction: Learners with Special Needs

- Look more closely at the federal Individuals with Disabilities Education Act website: http://idea.ed.gov/explore/home Select an area of interest; make notes about key insights and the classroom implications of these insights. Share these with colleagues.

- Think back to the beginning of your teaching career. What were you taught about working with students who have special needs in reading? Share these insights with colleagues, and together attempt to determine what advice is still appropriate and what, if anything, needs to be changed.

- Brainstorm with colleagues: Is the "special needs" label helpful? Why?

Chapter 1: Learners with Special Needs: What Does Research Tell Us?

- Write an explanation of Response to Intervention that you could use to explain the model to parents of learners with special needs. Read the explanation to your colleagues. Seek their feedback and, if warranted, make revisions.
- Talk with your colleagues about what may account for students' special needs in reading. Then form groups to make instructional plans for addressing each major reason. Share these with one another.
- Make a list of resource people in your school district. Talk with colleagues about when to contact resource people and how to work effectively with them to support children as readers.

Chapter 2: Assessing Learners with Special Needs

- Discuss each "big idea" about assessment in more detail. Decide if you agree or disagree with each, why, and what implications the ideas have for your classroom assessment plans for children with special needs in reading.
- List the possible revisions to your classroom assessment plans. Then rank order these. Explain your reasoning to your colleagues.
- For the most important revision idea from the activity above, develop an implementation plan. Share this with your colleagues and seek their feedback.

Chapter 3: Instructional Strategies for Teaching Learners with Special Needs

- Divide your group into pairs. Each pair should select one aspect of reading instruction (e.g., fluency, comprehension) and then (a) develop a goal for all students, (b) describe Tier 1 instruction, and (c) describe Tier 2 instruction. Be sure that instruction for both groups of students will enable them to accomplish the goal you have articulated.

- Brainstorm with colleagues to develop a list of ways to enhance social interaction during reading instruction. From the list, select two or three ways that are best suited to your instructional style. Explain these to your colleagues, and justify their selection.

- Using the two or three ideas you selected above, make concrete plans for implementing them. Seek feedback from colleagues and, if warranted, make revisions to your plans.

- For each idea selected above, make plans to assess impact. That is, how will you determine if these new activities are enhancing social interaction in your classroom? How will you determine if these ideas are benefiting students with special needs in reading?

Chapter 4: Beyond Strategies

- Go back to the ideas you generated about fostering social interaction in your classroom. Evaluate each idea in light of your English language learners (ELLs). Share your insights with colleagues.

- Together with colleagues, brainstorm school and community resources for fostering your relationships with ELLs' families.

- If you currently have an at-home reading program, evaluate its potential to support students with special needs in reading. You may find the guidelines described in the chapter helpful. Share the results of your evaluation with colleagues.

- If you do not currently have an at-home reading program, develop one. Again, you may find the guidelines described in the chapter helpful.

Phonemic Awareness and Phonics Resources

Common Rimes
(Phonograms or Word Families)

ab: tab, drab

ace: race, place

ack: lack, track

act: fact, pact

ad: bad, glad

ade: made, shade

aft: raft, craft

ag: bag, shag

age: page, stage

aid: maid, braid

ail: mail, snail

ain: rain, train

air: hair, stair

ait: bait, trait

ake: take, brake

alk: talk, chalk

all: ball, squall

am: ham, swam

ame: name, blame

arn: barn, yarn

arp: carp, harp

art: part, start

ase: base, case

ash: cash, flash

ask: mask, task

ass: lass, mass

at: fat, scat

atch: hatch, catch

ate: gate, plate

aught: caught, taught

ave: gave, shave

aw: saw, draw

awn: lawn, fawn

ax: wax, sax

ay: hay, clay

aze: haze, maze

ead: head, bread

eak: leak, sneak

eer: beer, peer

eet: feet, sleet

eg: leg, beg

eigh: weigh, sleigh

eight: weight, freight

ell: fell, swell

elt: felt, belt

en: Ben, when

end: tend, send

ent: sent, spent

ess: less, bless

est: rest, chest

et: get, jet

ew: flew, chew

ib: bib, crib

ibe: bribe, tribe

ice: rice, splice

ick: kick, stick

id: hid, slid

amp: camp, clamp
an: man, span
ance: dance, glance
and: land, gland
ane: plane, cane
ang: bang, sprang
ank: bank, plank
ant: pant, chant
ap: nap, snap
ape: tape, drape
ar: car, star
ard: hard, card
are: care, glare
ark: dark, spark
arm: harm, charm
ind: kind, blind
ine: mine, spine
ing: sing, string
ink: sink, shrink
ip: hip, flip
ipe: ripe, swipe
ire: tire, sire
irt: dirt, shirt
ise: rise, wise
ish: dish, swish
isk: disk, risk
iss: kiss, Swiss
ist: mist, wrist
it: hit, quit
itch: ditch, witch
ite: bite, write
ive: five, hive
ix: fix, six
o: do, to, who
o: go, no, so
oach: coach, poach
oad: road, toad
oal: coal, goal
oam: foam, roam
oan: Joan, loan
oar: boar, roar
oast: boast, coast
oat: boat, float

eal: real, squeal
eam: team, stream
ean: mean, lean
eap: heap, leap
ear: year, spear
eat: beat, cheat
eck: peck, check
ed: bed, shed
ee: tee, see
eed: need, speed
eek: leek, seek
eel: feel, knell
eem: deem, seem
een: seen, screen
eep: keep, sheep
old: gold, scold
ole: hole, stole
oll: droll, roll
ome: dome, home
one: cone, phone
ong: long, wrong
oo: too, zoo
ood: good, hood
ood: food, mood
ook: cook, took
ool: cool, fool
oom: room, bloom
oon: moon, spoon
oop: hoop, snoop
oot: boot, shoot
op: top, chop
ope: hope, slope
orch: porch, torch
ore: bore, snore
ork: cork, fork
orn: horn, thorn
ort: fort, short
oss: boss, gloss
ost: cost, lost
ost: host, most
ot: got, trot
otch: notch, blotch
ote: note, quote

ide: wide, pride
ie: die, pie
ief: thief, chief
ife: wife, knife
iff: cliff, whiff
ift: gift, sift
ig: pig, twig
ight: tight, bright
ike: Mike, spike
ile: mile, tile
ill: fill, chill
ilt: kilt, quilt
im: him, trim
in: tin, spin
ince: since, prince
ove: dove, love
ow: how, chow
ow: slow, throw
owl: howl, growl
own: down, town
own: known, grown
ox: fox, pox
oy: boy, ploy
ub: cub, shrub
uck: duck, stuck
ud: mud, thud
ude: dude, rude
udge: fudge, judge
ue: sue, blue
uff: puff, stuff
ug: dug, plug
ule: rule, mule
ull: dull, gull
um: sum, chum
umb: numb, thumb
ump: bump, plump
un: run, spun
une: June, tune
ung: hung, flung
unk: sunk, chunk
unt: bunt, hunt
ur: fur, blur
urn: burn, churn

104
....

APPENDIX B

*Phonemic
Awareness and
Phonics Resources*

ob: job, throb
obe: robe, globe
ock: lock, stock
od: rod, sod
ode: code, rode
og: fog, clog
oil: boil, broil
oin: coin, join
oke: woke, spoke

ough: rough, tough
ought: bought, brought
ould: could, would
ounce: bounce, pounce
ound: bound, found
ouse: house, mouse
out: pout, about
outh: mouth, south
ove: cove, grove

urse: curse, nurse
us: bus, plus
ush: mush, crush
ust: dust, trust
ut: but, shut
ute: lute, flute
y: my, dry

Mraz et al. (2008), pp. 64–65.

Action Phonics List

B:	bending, bouncing
C:	catching, calling, combing
D:	dancing, diving
F:	falling, filing, fixing
G:	galloping, gasping
H:	hopping, hiding, hitting
J:	jumping, juggling, jogging
K:	kicking, kissing
L:	laughing, licking, lunging
M:	marching, mixing, munching
N:	napping, nodding
P:	punching, pushing, painting
R:	running, resting, ripping
S:	saluting, sitting, singing
T:	talking, tickling, tapping
W:	wiggling, walking, waving
Y:	yawning, yelling
Z:	zipping, zigzagging

Mraz et al., 2008, p. 66.

Notes

This section can be used in several ways. As you work through the book, you may want to make notes here about important ideas gleaned from discussions. You can also keep track of additional resources. You may also want to use these pages to reflect upon changes you made in your instruction and to make notes about next steps.

General Issues and Ideas

Assessment Plans

Instructional Plans

APPENDIX C

Notes

Notes

Working with Home Partners

References

Allington, R. L. (1987, July/August). Shattered hopes: Why two federal reading programs have failed to correct reading failure. *Learning, 87,* 60–64.

Allington, R. L. (2000). *What really matters for struggling readers: Designing research-based programs.* New York, NY: Longman.

Allington, R. L. (2002). What I've learned about effective reading instruction. *Phi Delta Kappan, 83,* 740–747.

Allington, R. L., & McGill-Franzen, A. (1989). Different programs, indifferent instruction. In A. Gardner & D. Lipsky (Eds.), *Beyond separate education* (pp. 75–98). New York, NY: Brookes.

Allington, R. L., Stuetzel, H., Shake, M., & Lamarche, S. (1986). What is remedial reading? A descriptive study. *Reading Research and Instruction, 24,* 15–30.

Allington, R. L., & Walmsley, S. A. (Eds.). (1995). *No quick fix: Rethinking literacy programs in America's elementary schools.* New York, NY: Teachers College Press.

Beck, I. L., McKeown, M. G., & Kucan, L. (2002). *Bringing words to life: Robust vocabulary instruction.* New York, NY: Guilford.

Blachowicz, C. L. Z., & Fisher, P. (2006). *Teaching vocabulary in all classrooms* (3rd ed.). Upper Saddle River, NJ: Pearson/Merrill/Prentice Hall.

Brozo, W. (2009–2010). Response to Intervention or responsive instruction. *Journal of Adolescent and Adult Literacy, 53,* 277–281.

Burgess, S. R. (1999). The influence of speech perception, oral language ability, the home literacy environment, and prereading knowledge on the growth of phonological sensitivity: A 1-year longitudinal study. *Reading Research Quarterly, 34,* 400–402.

Clark, J. M., & Pavio, A. (1991). Dual coding theory and education. *Educational Psychology Review, 3,* 149–210.

Cooter, R., Marrin, P., & Mills-House, E. (1999). Family and community involvement: The bedrock of reading success. *The Reading Teacher, 52,* 891–896.

Cunningham, P. (1990). The Names Test: A quick assessment of decoding ability. *The Reading Teacher, 44,* 124–129.

Day, J., Dommer, K., Mraz, M., & Padak, N. (2002). *OhioReads: Tutor training plus manual.* Columbus, OH: Ohio Department of Education.

Demeris, H., Childs, R., & Jordan, A. (2007). The impact of students with special needs included in grade 3 classrooms on the large-scale achievement scores of students without special needs. *Canadian Journal of Education, 30,* 609–627.

Dufflemeyer, F. A., Kruse, A. E., Merkly, D. J., & Fyfe, S. A. (1994). Further validation and enhancement of the Names Test. *The Reading Teacher, 48,* 118–129.

Echevarria, J., Vogt, M., & Short, D. (2004). *Making content comprehensible for English learners: The SIOP model* (2nd ed.). Needham Heights, MA: Allyn & Bacon.

Education for All Handicapped Children Act of 1975. 20 U.S.C. § 401 (1975).

Fitzgerald, J., & Graves, M. (2004). *Scaffolding reading experiences for English-language learners.* Norwood, MA: Christopher Gordon.

Fuchs, D., & Fuchs, L. S. (1998). Treatment validity: A unifying concept for reconceptualizing the identification of learning disabilities. *Learning Disabilities Research and Practice, 13*(4), 204–219.

Fuchs, D., & Fuchs, L. S. (2005). Response to intervention: A blueprint for practitioners, policymakers, and parents. *Teaching Exceptional Children,* 57–61. Retrieved December 14, 2009, from http://www.caspsurveys.org/NEW/pdfs/rti0001.pdf

Fuchs, L. S. (2003). Assessing intervention responsiveness: Conceptual and technical issues. *Learning Disabilities Research and Practice, 18,* 172–186.

Gresham, F. M. (2002). Responsiveness to Intervention: An alternative approach to identification of learning disabilities. In R. Bradley, L. Danielson, & D. P. Hallahan (Eds.), *Identification of learning disabilities: Research to practice,* 467-564. Mahwah, NJ: Erlbaum.

Hasbrouck, J., & Tindal, G. (1992). Curriculum-based oral reading fluency norms for students in grades 2 through 5. *Teaching Exceptional Children, 24*(3), 41–44.

Hoff, K. E., & Robinson, S. L. (2002). Best practices in peer-mediated interventions. In A. Thomas & J. Grimes (Eds.), *Best practices in school psychology IV* (pp. 1555–1567). Bethesda, MD: National Association of School Psychologists.

Howe, K., & Shinn, M. (2001). *Standard reading assessment passages (RAPS) for use in general outcome measurements: A manual describing development and technical features.* Eden Prairie, MN: Edformations.

Hoyt, L. (1999). *Revisit, reflect, retell: Strategies for improving reading comprehension*. Portsmouth, NH: Heinemann.

Individuals with Disabilities Education Act Amendments of 2004, PL 108-446, 20 USC § 1400 *et seq*.

International Dyslexia Association. (2008). *Just the facts . . . Information provided by the International Dyslexia Association: Multisensory structured language teaching*. Baltimore, MD: Author.

Kim, A., Vaughn, S., Wanzek, J., & Wei, S. (2004). Graphic organizers and their effects on the reading comprehension of students with LD: A synthesis of the research. *Journal of Learning Disabilities, 37*(2), 105–118.

Krashen, S. (2004). *Free voluntary reading*. Retrieved February 16, 2010, from http://www.sdkrashen.com/articles/pac5

Martin, M. O., Mullis, I. V. S., & Kennedy, A. M. (Eds.). (2007). *PIRLS 2006 technical report*. Chestnut Hill, MA: TIMSS & PIRLS International Study Center, Boston College.

McTighe, J., & Wiggins, G. (2004). *Understanding by design*. Alexandria, VA: Association for Supervision and Curriculum Development.

Montague, M. (2008). Self-regulation strategies to improve mathematical problem solving for students with learning disabilities. *Learning Disability Quarterly, 31*(1), 37–44.

Mooney, P., Ryan, J. B., Uhing, B. M., Reid, R., & Epstein, M. H. (2005). A review of self-management interventions targeting academic outcomes for students with emotional and behavioral disorders. *Journal of Behavioral Education, 14*(3), 203–221.

Mraz, M., Padak, N., & Rasinski, T. (2008). *Evidence-based instruction in reading: A professional development guide to phonemic awareness*. Boston, MA: Pearson/Allyn & Bacon.

National Association of State Directors of Special Education (NASDE). (2006). *Response to Intervention: Policy considerations and implementation*. Alexandria, VA: Author.

National Reading Panel. (2000). *Report of the National Reading Panel: Teaching children to read: Report of the subgroups*. Washington, DC: U.S. Department of Health and Human Services, National Institutes of Health.

Newton, E., Padak, N., & Rasinski, T. (2008). *Evidence-based instruction in reading: A professional development guide to vocabulary instruction*. Boston, MA: Pearson/Allyn & Bacon.

Padak, N., & Rasinski, T. (2004a). Fast Start: A promising practice for family literacy programs. *Family Literacy Forum, 3*(2), 3–9.

Padak, N., & Rasinski, T. (2004b). Fast Start: Successful literacy instruction that connects homes and schools. In J. Dugan, P. Linder, M. B. Sampson, B. Brancato, & L. Elish-Piper (Eds.), *Celebrating the power of literacy, 2004 College Reading Association yearbook* (pp. 11–23). Logan, UT: College Reading Association.

Padak, N., & Rasinski, T. (2005). *Fast Start for early readers*. New York, NY: Scholastic.

Padak, N., & Rasinski, T. (2008). *Evidence-based instruction in reading: A professional development guide to fluency instruction*. Boston, MA: Pearson/Allyn & Bacon.

Palincsar, A. S. (1998). Social constructivist perspectives on teaching and learning. In J. T. Spence, J. M. Darley, & D. J. Foss (Eds.), *Annual review of psychology* (pp. 345–375). Palo Alto, CA: Annual Reviews.

Pinnell, G. S., Pikulski, J., Wixson, K., Campbell, J., Gough, P., & Beatty, A. (1995). *Listening to children read aloud*. Washington, DC: U.S. Department of Education, Office of Educational Research and Improvement.

Pressley, M. (2002). Effective beginning reading instruction. *Journal of Literacy Research, 34*, 165–188.

Rasinski, T. V. (2003). *The fluent reader: Oral reading strategies for building word recognition, fluency, and comprehension*. New York, NY: Scholastic.

Rasinski, T. V., & Padak, N. (2005a). *Three minute reading assessments: Word recognition, fluency, and comprehension for grades 1–4*. New York, NY: Scholastic.

Rasinski, T. V., & Padak, N. (2005b). *Three minute reading assessments: Word recognition, fluency, and comprehension for grades 5–8*. New York, NY: Scholastic.

Rasinski, T., & Padak, N. (2008a). *Evidence-based instruction in reading: A professional development guide to comprehension instruction*. Boston, MA: Pearson/Allyn & Bacon.

Rasinski, T., & Padak, N. (2008b). *From phonics to fluency* (2nd ed.). Boston, MA: Pearson/Allyn & Bacon.

Rasinski, T. V., Padak, N., & Fawcett, G. (2010). *Teaching children who find reading difficult* (4th ed.). New York, NY: Prentice Hall.

Rasinski, T. V., Padak, N. D., Linek, W. L., & Sturtevant, E. (1994). Effects of fluency development on urban second-grade readers. *Journal of Educational Research, 87*, 158–165.

Rasinski, T., Padak, N., Newton, R., & Newton, E. (2007). *Building vocabulary from word roots*. Huntington Beach, CA: Teacher Created Materials.

Rea, P. J., McLaughlin, V. L., & Walther-Thomas, C. (2002). Outcomes for students with learning disabilities in inclusive and pullout programs. *Exceptional Children, 68*, 203–222.

Reid, R., & Lienemann, T. O. (2006). *Strategy instruction for students with learning disabilities*. New York, NY: Guilford Press.

Ryan, J., Reid, R., & Epstein, M. (2004). Peer-mediated intervention studies on academic achievement for students with EBD. *Remedial and Special Education, 25*, 330–341.

Salonen, R., Vauras, M., & Efklides, A. (2005). Social interaction—What can it tell us about metacognition and coregulation in learning? *European Psychologist, 10*(3), 199–208.

Scruggs, T. E., & Mastropieri, M. A. (2002). On babies and bathwater: Addressing the problems of identification of learning disabilities. *Learning Disability Quarterly, 25*, 155–168.

Senechal, M., LeFevre, J., & Thomas, E. (1998). Differential effects of home literacy experiences on the development of oral and written language. *Reading Research Quarterly, 33*, 96–116.

Snow, C. E., Griffin, P., & Burns, M. S. (2005). *Knowledge to support the teaching of reading: Preparing teachers for a changing world.* San Francisco, CA: Jossey-Bass.

Spencer, S., & Logan, K. (2005). Improving students with learning disabilities ability to acquire and generalize a vocabulary learning strategy. *Learning Disabilities: A Multidisciplinary Journal, 13*(3), 87–94.

Stanovich, K. E., & Siegal, L. S. (1994). Phenotypic performance profiles of children with reading disabilities: A regression-based test of phonological-core variable-difference model. *Journal of Educational Psychology, 86*, 24–53.

Stevenson, B., Rasinski, T., & Padak, N. (2006). Teaching fluency (and decoding) through Fast Start. In T. Rasinski, C. Blachowicz, & K. Lems (Eds.), *Teaching reading fluency* (pp. 253–264). New York, NY: Guilford.

Taffe, S., Fisher, P. J., & Blachowicz, C. L. Z. (2009). Vocabulary instruction for diverse students. In. L. M. Morrow, R. Rueda, & D. Lapp (Eds.), *Handbook of research on literacy instruction: Issues of diversity, policy, and equity* (pp. 320–336). New York, NY: Guilford.

Taylor, E., & Collins, V. (2003). *Literacy leadership for grades 5–12.* Alexandria, VA: Association for Supervision and Curriculum Development.

Tierney, R. (1998). Literacy assessment reform: Shifting beliefs, principled possibilities, and emerging practices. *The Reading Teacher, 51*, 374–390.

U.S. Department of Education. (2005). *Twenty-seventh annual report to Congress on the implementation of the Education of the Handicapped Act.* Washington, DC: U.S. Government Printing Office.

U.S. Department of Education, Office of Educational Research and Improvement, National Center for Education Statistics. (2001). *Fourth-grade reading highlights 2000.* Washington, DC: U.S. Department of Education, Office of Educational Research and Improvement.

Vaughn, S., & Fuchs, L. S. (2003). Redefining learning disabilities as inadequate response to instruction: The promise and potential problems. *Learning Disabilities Research and Practice, 18*(3), 137–146.

Vygotsky, L. S. (1978). *Mind in society* (M. Cole, V. John-Steiner, S. Scribner, & E. Souberman, Eds.). Cambridge, MA: Harvard University Press.

West, K. (1998). Noticing and responding to learners: Literacy evaluation and instruction in the primary grades. *The Reading Teacher, 51,* 550–559.

Wisniewski, R., Fawcett, G., Padak, N., & Rasinski, T. (in press). *Evidence-based instruction in reading: A professional development guide to culturally responsive instruction.* Upper Saddle River, NJ: Pearson.

Yopp, H. K. (1995). A test for assessing phonemic awareness in young children. *The Reading Teacher, 49,* 20–29.

Zimmerman, B., Padak, N., & Rasinski, T. (2008). *Evidence-based instruction in reading: A professional development guide to phonics instruction.* Boston, MA: Pearson/Allyn & Bacon.

Children's Books Cited

Numeroff, L. (1985). *If you give a mouse a cookie.* New York, NY: HarperCollins.

Schultz, C. (2002). *A Charlie Brown Thanksgiving.* New York, NY: Random House.

Thaler, M., & Lee, J. (2003). *The class pet from the black lagoon.* New York, NY: Scholastic.